POINT COUNT BIDDING
in Contract Bridge

BY

CHARLES H. GOREN

Eyre & Spottiswoode

LONDON

First published 1950
Revised edition 1953
Reprinted   1954
Reprinted   1955
Reprinted   1956
Reprinted   1958

Catalogue No. 6/2215

This book is printed in Great Britain for Eyre & Spottiswoode
(Publishers) Ltd., 15 Bedford Street, London, W.C.2, by
Lowe & Brydone (Printers) Limited, London, N.W.10

POINT COUNT BIDDING

TABLE OF CONTENTS

INTRODUCTION

Background to the Point Count Method of Bidding

FOR A GREAT many years I have advocated the point count for all phases of No Trump bidding, and to a limited extent where trump suits were involved. It may have been surprising to many of my readers therefore that I should have delayed so long publishing a book on the point count for suit bidding, though it became apparent that a great many players in all parts of the continent found this method of presentation so much to their tastes.

The answer is a simple one. As I have ofttimes stated, I never ask my students to serve as guinea pigs. Consequently I determined to postpone publication of my complete work until such time as I was able to cure most of the defects and iron out many of the fallacies that were inherent in the different versions of the point count method that had heretofore been hastily offered to the public in various parts of this country and England.

It required a great deal of study and experimentation. But, with the assistance of William M. Anderson of Toronto, head of one of Canada's foremost life insurance companies and an actuary of great renown, I was able to develop a scale of values which will work effectively in an overwhelming majority of hands.

Before we proceed any further, let me make it clear that the POINT COUNT is not a SYSTEM. It is an approach; a simplified method for valuing one's hand. So you are not to feel that a new system is being foisted upon you. The bidding methods which I advocate, and which are currently employed by a majority of players both in this country and abroad, remain substantially intact.

Extravagant claims have been put forth by numerous contributors for the merits of the point count and sharp attacks have been made upon the efficiency of the other methods. These views I do not share. I do not believe the point count will do away with tattletale gray. Nor am I persuaded that anyone with an abacus can become a Bridge expert in less time than it takes to get a degree from Arthur Murray's Cathedral of Learning. I only contend that in bidding this way you will make fewer mistakes than you did before.

To those few who still remain devotees of the honor trick table, I say in all sincerity, in adopting the methods herein advocated you need sacrifice none of your convictions, compromise with none of your loyalties nor change your way of life. I am not an evangelist, and it is not my purpose to win anyone over to the true faith. You will, therefore, find here no scathing attack upon those who employ methods other than my own.

There is recommended to you, here, a more delicate method of valuation than has been employed through the years of Contract. In measurements of any kind, the use of feet and inches, instead of yards, permits the achievement of greater refinement without imposing too heavy a burden on the student. If you will overcome the slight mental hazard of the larger figures, you will find this method very easy to work with; for after a while you will see that it follows a distinct and logical pattern.

My table may appear at first blush to be slightly more complicated than others that have previously been published. Actually it isn't. To be sure, I could have made it a bit simpler, but only at the expense of accuracy which I am sure you would not choose to sacrifice.

The basis of this method is my old ditty: "An opening bid facing an opening bid will produce game." Translated into figures, a partnership holding of 26 points will normally produce game.

Now every time you have 26 points, I don't want you to go out and hock your Grandpa's portrait to make a bet with the local bookmaker on coming home with the game. Many a 26 pointer has gone down to defeat. Such mishap should be accepted with equanimity. The finger of scorn is not to be pointed at some unfortunate player to the tune of, "There goes a man with 26 points who failed to contract for game!" Nor should the scarlet letter be branded upon the forehead of an otherwise virtuous young lady, who contracted for game with somewhat less than the required count only to be set a trick or two.

We still allow sway for the human factor as will be evident in my treatment of those twilight zones, which I refer to as judgment points.

It is appropriate to make acknowledgment, here, to all those who have contributed both directly and indirectly to this effort. Particularly to Victor Mollo, an Englishman who wrote one of the early works on the subject. While I cannot see eye to eye with many of his theories, there is no doubt that he did considerable pioneering in the field, and *his scholarly treatise* (Streamlined Bridge) *provided the basis for many of my experiments. Above all, to William M. Anderson, who not only is the last word where mathematical problems are concerned, but whose broad understanding of the fundamental theories of the game I was able to put to very practical use.*

CHARLES H. GOREN

NOTE TO THE READER: *If you have already had experience with a point count method in No Trump bidding, it may be advisable for you to begin this book by reviewing Chapter IV before you turn to Chapter I.*

Opening Bids of One in a Suit

THE POINT COUNT TABLE

ACE = 4 POINTS

KING = 3 POINTS

QUEEN = 2 POINTS

JACK = 1 POINT

The Pack contains 40 points*

An average hand is 10 points

Unprotected honors should be discounted. Where the King is unguarded (alone) it should be reduced from 3 to 2. The unguarded Queen (Q or Qx) should be reduced from 2 to 1, and the singleton Jack should be regarded as a singleton spot card. However, the reduction should not be made in cases where partner has bid the suit.

Note that while the value of the unguarded honor changes, the distributional points always remain constant. Deduct a point for an Aceless hand. Add a point if a hand contains four Aces.

THE VALUE of a hand for purposes of opening the bidding is computed by adding the high card point count to the *points assigned for distribution*. The points assigned for distribution are as follows:

ADD 3 POINTS FOR A VOID

ADD 2 POINTS FOR EACH SINGLETON

ADD 1 POINT FOR EACH DOUBLETON

Requirements

If your hand contains 12 points you may open if you have a good rebid and two quick tricks in your hand.

*While for No Trump bidding the pack remains constant at 40 points, it will be seen that there can be no such constant figure for suit bidding.

If your hand contains 13 points you have an optional opening and you may open if you feel like it.

If your hand contains 14 points it must be opened!

Since the allowance of value for short suits in the opening
hand will appear to be a departure from long established
theories, let us examine briefly how it works.

♠ A K 10 x x (7)
♡ A x x   (4)
◇ x x x
♣ x x   (1)

This hand contains only 12 points but since it has a convenient rebid of 2 Spades it should be opened. It will be
noted that a point is allowed for the doubleton Club. This
produces the same result as though a point had been allowed instead for the fifth Spade, a practice which has been
followed by most writers who have previously written on
the point count. If the result appears to be the same, why
then, the reader may ask, do I use a different method?

The answer is simple: by counting only the fifth and
sixth card of your long suit certain distributional advan-
tages are completely lost. Take these two hands:

(A) ♠ A K 10 x x   (B) ♠ A K 10 x x
      ♡ A x x   ♡ A x x x
      ◇ x x x   ◇ x x
      ♣ x x   ♣ x x

Which one is better? Definitely hand (B). What is the mar-
gin of superiority? The fourth heart, for which some writers
have not made allowance. By assigning a point for each of

the doubletons, we reach a value of 13 points for hand (B) compared with 12 for hand (A). What I have really done is allow a point for the fifth Spade and a point for the fourth Heart, but that would be too much work, and much too difficult to remember. It is much simpler to reach the precise answer by counting the short suits. This takes care of all distributions.

Let us see how that principle applies to four card suits:

♠ A x x x (4)
♡ A x x (4)
◇ A x x (4)
♣ x x x

This hand contains 12 points but has no convenient rebid. So it should be passed.

♠ A 10 x x (4)
♡ A x x x (4)
◇ A x x   (4)
♣ x x   (1)

This hand contains 13 points and is an optional opening. If you feel like bidding, open with 1 Spade intending to rebid 2 Hearts if partner responds 2 Clubs. If this doesn't put you at your mental ease, exercise your option by refusing to open the bidding.

♠ A 10 x x (4)
♡ A x x x (4)
◇ x   (2)
♣ A x x x (4)

This hand contains 14 points and must be opened.

It will be seen that if only the fifth card in a suit is taken into consideration the following three hands would all have the same value.

(A)	(B)	(C)
♠ A 10 x x	♠ A 10 x x	♠ A 10 x x
♡ A x x	♡ A x x x	♡ A x x x
◊ A x x	◊ A x x	◊ x
♣ x x x	♣ x x	♣ A x x x

This is obviously unsound. By assigning distributional points, 1 point for a doubleton, 2 points for a singleton, we arrive at the accurate valuation of these hands:

$$(A)—12 \qquad (B)—13 \qquad (C)—14$$

Let us see how this works with two suiters.

♠ A Q x x x	(6)
♡ A 10 x x x	(4)
◊ x x	(1)
♣ x	(2)

I think your instinct will tell you that this hand should *be* opened. Our experience convinces us that such action is mandatory. In high cards the hand contains only 10 points. If only the fifth Spade were taken into consideration the hand would have a value of 11 points, and would be an obvious pass. But, allowing 2 points for the singleton and 1 point for the doubleton brings the value of the hand to 13 points. Since an easy rebid of 2 Hearts is available, the hand should be opened with 1 Spade.

The soundness of this doctrine becomes apparent with a slight rearrangement of the above hand:

(A)	(B)
♠ A Q x x x	♠ A Q x x x
♡ A 10 x x x	♡ A 10 x
◇ x x	◇ x x x
♣ x	♣ x x

Hand (A) is obviously 2 points better than hand (B). Counting the singleton and doubleton has not only permitted us to reach the exact valuation for the hand, but has actually lightened our mental burden, in the sense that it did some of our thinking for us.

Notice that hand (A) undergoes no change in value if the two short suits are combined to produce a void suit, e.g.,

♠ A Q x x x	(6)
♡ A 10 x x x	(4)
◇ x x x	
♣ none	(3)

The hand retains a value of 13 points.

Examine the following hands containing four card suits:

(A)	(B)	(C)
♠ A J x x (5)	♠ A J x x (5)	♠ A x x x (4)
♡ A K x x (7)	♡ A K x (7)	♡ K J x x (4)
◇ x x x	◇ J x x (1)	◇ x (2)
♣ x x (1)	♣ x x x	♣ K J x x (4)
13	13	14

Hand (A) contains 13 points which makes it an optional opening. The option in this case should be exercised because a convenient rebid is available if you open with 1 Spade. Partner responds 2 Clubs, and you are in a position conveniently to rebid 2 Hearts. Hand (B) also contains 13 points but the option to bid need not be exercised since there is no convenient rebid. Hand (C) contains 14 points and is therefore a mandatory opening of 1 Club.

To repeat, where a hand contains only one long suit the addition of 1 point for the fifth and 1 point for the sixth card will produce accurate results, but where a second suit is held such valuation will be false. Such methods will also prove faulty when three suits are held. (See Page 11 for examples of this type of hand.)

1 Club Opening

There is a common misconception that this is a system or convention. Nothing could be farther from the truth. The short Club bid is used to open the bidding on hands that contain 15 points or less but offer no other convenient opening or rebid. A 1 Club opening always makes it easy to rebid for if worse comes to worst opener may rebid 1 No Trump.

(A)		(B)	
♠ A K Q x	(9)	♠ 10 x x x	
♡ x x x		♡ J x x x	(1)
◇ x x x		◇ K x	(3)
♣ A J x	(5)	♣ A K Q	(9)
		1 for the	
		doubleton	(1)
	14		14

Both these hands are mandatory openings. In hand (A) if you open 1 Spade, an awkward situation develops if partner responds 2 Hearts or 2 Diamonds. Therefore, bid 1 Club.

In hand (B) no biddable suit is available so the bidding should be opened with 1 Club.

Third Position Openings

In third position, the bidding may be opened with as little as 11 points. In fact, with an understanding partner, I may shade the requirements to 10 points where a good suit is held. The reason for relaxing the requirements is that the third hand opener is not required to make a rebid. He has a passing partner, and even if responder names a new suit, the third hand bidder need not go on.

$$
\begin{array}{lll}
\spadesuit & \text{A K J x x} & (8) \\
\heartsuit & \text{Q x x} & (2) \\
\diamondsuit & \text{x x x} & \\
\clubsuit & \text{x x} & \underline{(1)} \\
& & 11
\end{array}
$$

This hand should be opened in third position with a bid of 1 Spade.

Opening bidder, in this case, need not bid again, for it is reasonable to presume that a passing bidder will not contribute 14 points, so that the partnership cannot have the 26 points needed for game.

Fourth Position Openings

The requirements for a fourth hand opening bid are the same as for first and second hand. There is one distinction. Opener need not be prepared to rebid, inasmuch as his partner passed originally.

♠ A Q x x   (6)
♡ A K x   (7)
◇ x x x
♣ x x x

——
13

This is a good opening in fourth position, (13 points), though it would not be acceptable for first or second hand, because a convenient rebid is not available.

Choice of Suits

The use of the point count for hand valuation has no effect on the established rules about which suit to bid first. The rules remain as always.

With two five card suits bid the higher ranking first (with some exceptions, where five Spades and five Clubs are held).

With a five and a four card suit bid the five card suit first. (See exceptions.)

With a six-five, bid the six card suit first, then bid the five card suit twice.

With four card suits start with the suit that ranks next below your singleton or doubleton.

EXCEPTIONS:

Treat any weak five card suit as though it were a four card suit when this will create a convenient rebid—for example:

♠ Q x x x x
♡ K x x
◇ x
♣ A K J x

Treating the weak five card Spade suit as though it were a four card suit, it would then be proper to open with the suit below the singleton, i.e., 1 Club.

Example:

You hold:

♠ K x x x x
♡ x
◇ x x
♣ A K J x x

For the sake of convenience this hand is opened with 1 Club. A Spade opening would prove awkward if partner responds 2 Hearts or 2 Diamonds, for no convenient rebid is available. The hand is not strong enough for a rebid at the level of 3 Clubs; therefore you would find yourself in the position of having to rebid 2 Spades on a non-rebiddable suit.

Exception to the five-four rule: With hands of moderate strength, particularly where your suits are next-door-neighbors in rank, the hand should be treated as though the suits were of equal length. For example, as dealer you hold:

♠ A K J x
♡ K Q x x x
◇ x x
♣ x x

This is a hand of moderate strength and the suits are next-door-neighbors. It is better to make believe that your Spades and Hearts are the same length. Therefore, open the bidding with 1 Spade, providing an easy rebid of 2 Hearts over partner's response.

As dealer you hold:

> ♠ A K x x
> ♡ A K x x x
> ◇ K x
> ♣ x x

Here the opening bidder's hand has great strength (19 points) and should be bid naturally, that is, the five card suit first. The proper opening bid is 1 Heart. Over a bid of 2 Clubs you are well prepared to rebid 2 Spades. This is equivalent to bidding at the level of 3, which requires a good hand. This hand qualifies as such inasmuch as it is valued at 19 points, 17 in high cards and 2 for distribution (1 for each doubleton). The requirements for a reverse may occasionally be shaded to 18 points.

On three-suited hands that are valued at 20 points or more, and where the text book opening bid would be 1 Spade, it is good tactics to open exceptionally with 1 of a minor suit in order to make it easy for partner to respond, for example:

As dealer you hold:

> ♠ A K x x
> ♡ A Q x x
> ◇ K Q 10 x
> ♣ x

This hand is valued at 20 points (18 in high cards and 2 for the singleton Club). The normal opening is 1 Spade, the suit below the singleton. However, partner would not respond to a bid of 1 Spade if he held the following hand:

♠ x x
♡ K J 10 x x
◇ x x x
♣ x x x

for it possesses only 4 points in high cards and does not qualify as a 1 No Trump response.* But if the opening bid is 1 Diamond, responder may make a shaded response of 1 Heart. For purposes of bidding a suit his hand is valued at 5 points (4 in high cards and 1 for the doubleton).

EXAMPLES of long-card hands. Do not regard these values for doubletons, singletons and voids as ruffing values. On the contrary, they represent long cards. If a hand contains a doubleton, it must hold one long card; if it contains a singleton, it must hold two long cards; if it contains a void, it must hold three long cards.

Now, what are long cards? You start counting your long cards from the fifth card of the trump suit and the fourth card of any side suit. For example:

(A)	(B)
♠ A K x x x	♠ A x x x
♡ A x x x	♡ x
◇ x x x	◇ A K J x
♣ x	♣ K x x x

On Hand (A) the opening bid is 1 Spade. It is worth 13 points, 11 points in high cards, one for the fifth Spade (trumps) and one for the fourth Heart (a side suit).

On Hand (B) the opening bid is 1 Diamond. It is worth 17 points, 15 points in high cards and two for distribution—1 for the fourth Spade (a side suit), 1 for the fourth Club (a side suit), but no point is assigned for length in Diamonds. That is the trump suit, and we count length in the trump suit only from the fifth card.

When I first presented this technique to the public in 1949, this was the method employed, that is, counting long cards. Students were told to add 1 point for each trump over four, and 1 point for each card over three in any side suit. This was the Rule of 3 and 4.

You may have observed how cumbersome it is to count these long cards. My students found it so, and since exactly the same result is obtained by adding 1 point for each doubleton, 2 points for each singleton and 3 points for a void, I substituted the simpler formula, which was universally accepted throughout the country and has now become standard.

*See page 44 on responses.

CHAPTER II

Opening Two Bids

ONE of the gratifying things about the presentation of this point count is that I am in a position to offer a cure for a malady that has been ravaging Bridge communities for almost two decades. I refer to the epidemic type of two demand bids. To say that this convention is generally abused is to put it with extreme mildness. And the ailment knows no geographical boundaries. From under the shadow of the Empire State Building to the Yosemite Valley you will find players bursting into a two demand bid any time they catch a glimpse of anything resembling 5½ honor tricks.

From time to time various formulae have been prescribed for the player who prefers not to think it out for himself. In the early, uninformed days of Contract the price was fixed at 5½ honor tricks and a biddable suit. That's the one that did all the damage, and it left its mark for another generation.

Then came the formula that read, "You must have more honor tricks than losers." This seemed confusing.

Then followed the rule of 13, which I never quite mastered.

But despite all these one still heard "The Song of the Two Bid." I don't know how the tune runs but the lyrics have fastened themselves in my memory. Here's the opening line of the chorus: "I can't understand it, partner; I had 5½ honor tricks."

My own formula was perhaps the simplest of all. You must have game in hand (almost). That is to say, if you open 2 Spades, you should be able to win at least nine tricks in your own hand, and your hand must contain at least four high card tricks. This, I believe, was the most successful of all in bringing light to the community.

It was easy to use on solid hands such as:

♠ A K Q J x x x
♡ A x
♢ x
♣ A x x

but a little more difficult on hands with scattered strength; like this:

♠ A K J x x
♡ A
♢ A K x
♣ K Q 10 x

It has been suggested that the point count is of no practical use for two bids. This I must deny vehemently, for we have it now. There is good reason to be confident that the newly devised formula will put an end to the sewing circle two bid. A student following this method can hardly go wrong. The point count actually does some of his thinking for him.

The requirements for an opening two demand bid are in brief as follows:

A. With a good five card suit, about 25 points

B. With a good six card suit, about 23 points

C. With a good seven card suit, about 21 points

D. With a second good five card suit, 1 point less than above

See how this works:

	(A)		(B)
♠ A K J x x	(8)	♠ A K Q J x x	(10)
♡ A	(4)	♡ A K x	(7)
◊ A K x	(7)	◊ A x	(4)
♣ K Q 10 x	(5)	♣ x x	
2 for singleton	(2)	1 for each doubleton	(2)
	26		23

	(C)
♠ A K Q J x x x	(10)
♡ A x	(4)
◊ x	
♣ A x x	(4)
2 for the singleton	
1 for the doubleton	(3)
	21

Open 2 Spades on all these hands.
(A) A good 5 card suit with 26 points
(B) A good 6 card suit with 23 points
(C) A good 7 card suit with 21 points

This will shield the student from the temptation of opening with a two bid on the following hand:

♠ A Q x x x	(6)
♡ A K x	(7)
◊ A K x	(7)
♣ x x	
1 for doubleton	(1)
	21

This hand, it will be seen, has the value of only 21 points and does not approach an opening two demand bid. It should be opened with 1 Spade, and if partner does not keep the bidding open do not be concerned about having missed a game.

When opening with a two bid, it is discreet to assume that partner is trickless, or virtually so. Accordingly, if you have any insufficiently guarded honors in short suits, it is sound practice not to count them, since you must assume that they will fall to opponent's high cards. Holdings like J x or Q x had better be discounted entirely when contemplating a two demand bid.

The requirements for two bids as stated above assume that there is a good chance that the hand is to be played in a major suit or No Trump. If it seems that your hand must play in a minor suit, the requirements should be increased by 2 points.

Conversely, where you have a good major two suiter, you may occasionally relax the requirements by a point or two.

CHAPTER III

Opening Pre-Emptive Bids

OPENING pre-emptive bids are not made with good hands. Their sole purpose is to discommode the enemy. Any hand containing more than two quick tricks should not be opened with a pre-empt. To put it in another way: Do not pre-empt on any hand that contains as many as 11 points in high cards (exclusive of distribution).

The following hands may be opened with pre-emptive bids of 3 Spades:

♠ K Q J 10 x x x x   ♠ Q J 10 x x x x x
♡ x x   ♡ x x
◊ x x   ◊ A x
♣ x   ♣ x

In fact, when not vulnerable, good results may be obtained by opening such hands with 4 Spades. They each possess 7 winners, safeguarding the opener against any great disaster.

IN BRIEF

The value of a hand is determined by computing the high cards held, and adding:

> 3 points for a void
>
> 2 points for each singleton
>
> 1 point for each doubleton

———

12 point hands may be opened if there is a *good* rebid, and the hand contains two quick tricks.

13 point hands are optional openings. Bid them if convenient.

14 point hands *must* be opened.

———

A third hand opening may be made with 11 points if a fairly good suit is held.

A fourth hand opening should be made on 13 points, even though no good rebid is available.

———

An opening demand bid of 2 in a suit requires:

A good five card suit with a minimum of 25 points

A good six card suit with a minimum of 23 points

A good seven card suit with a minimum of 21 points

———

Do not make an opening pre-emptive bid on any hand containing as many as 11 points (exclusive of distribution).

CHAPTER IV

The Point Count
as it applies to
No Trump Bidding

OPENING NO TRUMP BIDS

ACE = 4 POINTS
KING = 3 POINTS
QUEEN = 2 POINTS
JACK = 1 POINT

The Pack contains 40 points

With hands containing all four Aces, add 1 point.

IT IS highly desirable to keep this figure 40 constant. It is for this reason that it is better practice, in No Trump, not to assign points for distribution; for if each partner does so, a deal might contain as many as 76 points. The advantage of retaining the 40 points as a constant is this: When you can count your assets to 37, you know for a certainty that the opposition cannot hold an Ace, for they have only 3 points between them.

However, I do recognize the value of a five card suit, but I obtain distributional values by a slightly different approach. A raise from 1 No Trump to 2 No Trump requires 8 points; but you may raise with 7 points if you have a reasonably good five card suit or if you have good intermediate cards.

A raise from 1 No Trump to 3 No Trump requires 10 points, but you may do it with 9 if you have a five card suit. It's just as easy and keeps the numbers even. To put it in another way: with five card suits the requirements for raises and rebids are lowered by a point.

---

26 points will normally produce 3 No Trump

33 points will normally produce 6 No Trump

37 points will normally produce 7 No Trump

OPENING 1 NO TRUMP BIDS

The requirements for an open 1 No Trump bid are:

(1) The point count must be between 16 and 18

(2) The hand must be balanced, that is

4-3-3-3
4-4-3-2
5-3-3-2

with the proviso that the doubleton should be headed by a high honor

(3) At least three suits must be protected

Hands counting 19, 20 and 21 are too big for 1 No Trump and must be opened with 1 of a suit. On the second round opener will make a jump rebid in No Trump.

The question is frequently raised, why are hands counting 19, 20 and 21 too big for 1 No Trump? The reason is to be found in our requirements for raises. If your partner opens with 1 No Trump and you have a balanced hand, 8 points are required for a raise. If you have only 6 or 7, you should pass.

If partner has opened 1 No Trump with 20 or 21 points and you have passed with 6 or 7, the partnership may possess as many as 28 points; yet the hand will be played in 1 No Trump. If the opening bid, instead, is 1 of a suit, partner will respond at the level of 1 with as little as 6 points. Opener may then jump in No Trump, knowing that the partnership probably has the necessary 26 points.

Not infrequently I have observed players making a 1 No Trump bid on hands like this:

     ♠ K Q x x
     ♡ A J x x
     ◊ A
     ♣ K x x x

"I had 17 points," they announce, as though standing upon their rights.

A 1 No Trump opening must not only have the right SIZE, but it must have the right SHAPE.

No Trump openings *must* be made on a balanced hand, that is: 4-3-3-3 — 4-4-3-2 — 5-3-3-2. Never on 4-4-4-1.

There are a great many advanced players who make it a practice to open some 19 point hands with 1 No Trump. The purpose is to avoid certain problems in rebidding.

Examine the following four cases:

(A)	(B)	(C)	(D)
♠ K x	♠ A x x	♠ K J x	♠ A Q x
♡ A Q x	♡ A Q x	♡ A Q x	♡ A Q x
◇ K Q x x	◇ A Q x x	◇ K J x x	◇ A J x
♣ K Q x x	♣ Q J x	♣ K Q x	♣ Q x x x

A number of the leading players preferred to open with 1 No Trump at risk of missing a good play for game if partner held 7 points without a five-card suit. The reason assigned was that they wished to avoid a 2 No Trump rebid if partner responded with 2 Hearts—a rebid which would be rather uncomfortable on hands (A) and (B). They also observed that if they opened with one of a suit and partner responded 1 No Trump they would be obliged to raise to two, so that if partner happened to have made a shaded response they would needlessly be playing at 2 No Trump instead of one, which responder would have passed. Furthermore, if a 19 point balanced hand is opened with one of a suit, and partner responds with one of some other suit, it becomes mandatory for opener to jump to 2 No Trump. Now if responder has taken the liberty of making a shaded response with less than 6 points in high cards, he will pass 2 No Trump, but you will find yourself as opener in a shaky contract for eight tricks when you could have purchased the hand a stage lower by opening with 1 No Trump. The points saved on hands of this character, they contend, compensate for those games which they occasionally miss by opening 19 point No Trump.

However, for the vast majority of players it is recommended that the limits of the 1 No Trump opening be kept strictly within the figures 16 and 18 inclusive. This rule has the benefit of simplicity and will be welcomed by teachers, who will find that their students will have an easier time committing the pattern to memory. Each division of No Trump bids will contain exactly three figures.

1 No Trump	16-17-18
Too big for 1 No Trump	19-20-21
2 No Trump	22-23-24
3 No Trump	25-26-27

Observe that it is never my purpose to speak as one who has achieved a scoop. I have no special admiration for originality or novelty where Bridge methods are concerned. Bridge systems, like shoes, give better service after they have been broken-in.

This system is recommended for your personal use. I use it myself, having learned about its soundness at the cost of a misspent youth.

Opening Bid of 2 No Trump

The requirements for an opening bid of 2 No Trump are:

(1) The point count must be between 22 and 24

(2) The hand must be balanced in distribution

(3) All four suits must be protected

An opening bid of 2 No Trump is not forcing. Partner may pass if he lacks the necessary values to raise.

Opening Bid of 3 No Trump

The requirements for an opening bid of 3 No Trump are:

(1) The point count must be between 25 and 27

(2) The hand must be balanced in distribution

(3) All four suits must be protected

CHAPTER V

Responses to No Trump Bids

CONSTANTLY bear in mind that it takes approximately 26 points to make a game at No Trump. When a five card suit is held, 25 points will usually be sufficient.

Permit me to inject a cheerful note by reminding you that 33 or 34 points will normally produce a small slam. (Opponents cannot have two Aces, since their high card strength is limited to 7 points.) And I trust that it will be of more than academic interest to you that 37 or 38 should yield a grand slam. (Opponents cannot have an Ace, since their maximum high card holding is 3 points.)

In many cases responder can tell at a glance what the total partnership assets amount to. This is done by simple arithmetic. For the opener, by his opening bid of 1 No Trump, 2 No Trump, or 3 No Trump, has announced almost exactly how many points he has.

Responding to an
Opening Bid of 1 No Trump

When responder holds a balanced hand

When partner opens with 1 No Trump and you have a 5-3-3-2, there is no advantage in showing your suit. Raise the No Trump if you have the required count.

Raise to 2 No Trump with 8 or 9 points. (You may raise with 7 points if you have a five card suit.)

Raise to 3 No Trump with 10 to 14 points.

Raise to 4 No Trump with 15 or 16 points.

Raise to 6 No Trump with 17 or 18 points.

If you hold 19 or 20 points, a bid of 6 No Trump is not quite adequate. First make a jump shift to 3 of some suit, and then follow up with 6 No Trump. Showing a suit and jumping to 6 No Trump is a little stronger action than just jumping to 6 No Trump.

Raise to 7 No Trump with 21 or more, for then your partnership is assured of at least 37 points.

When responder holds an unbalanced hand

A response of 2 in a minor suit denies the ability to raise in No Trump, and therefore shows less than 7 points. A responder who has the high card values for a raise to 2 No Trump must in no circumstances respond with 2 Clubs or 2 Diamonds. Even if his hand contains a singleton he should raise the No Trump.

A takeout to 2 of a minor is made either

(a) on a hand that has no prospect for game, but contains a long suit in which the hand obviously must play, or

(b) on a hand which is just short of the requirements for a raise. That is, a hand with a five card suit and 6 points.

Takeout to 2 Hearts or 2 Spades

This bid must be distinguished from a takeout to 2 of a minor. For it may be made on a hand that contains 8 points, but one that is unbalanced and where you have some mental reservations as to whether the hand will play better at a suit or at No Trump.

Partner opens with 1 No Trump and you hold:

        ♠ K J x x x
        ♡ A x x x
        ◇ x
        ♣ x x x

Your hand contains 8 points in high cards and qualifies as a raise to 2 No Trump. However, because of the unbalanced nature of your holding, the hand may play better in Spades, and the cooperation of your partner is solicited in making the decision. You respond 2 Spades; if partner raises to 3 Spades you will prefer the Spade game. If partner rebids 2 No Trump you will raise to 3 No Trump.

Had your holding been:

        ♠ x
        ♡ x x x
        ◇ A x x x
        ♣ K J x x x

your proper response would have been 2 No Trump, not 2 Clubs. For your hand contains 8 points in high cards and qualifies as a raise. There is now no sound choice between 5 Clubs and 3 No Trump. Whereas in the preceding example there was a real choice between 4 Spades and 3 No Trump.

Similarly if you held:

♠ K J x x x
♡ x x
♢ A x x
♣ x x x

Holding a balanced hand you should favor No Trump rather than a suit and should raise to 2 No Trump instead of bidding 2 Spades.

A response of 2 Hearts or 2 Spades may also be made on hopeless hand with a long suit, e.g.,

♠ J x x x x x x
♡ x x
♢ J x x
♣ x

Partner opens with 1 No Trump. You respond 2 Spades. If he rebids 2 No Trump you rebid 3 Spades, and he must pass.

To recapitulate: Where the bidding has proceeded

Opener	Responder
1 No Trump	2 Clubs

Opener will usually pass, and must do so, unless he has at least 18 points.

Opener	Responder
1 No Trump	2 Spades

Opener will usually bid again, and should do so, unless he has opened with just 16 points and no distributional advantage in favor of Spades.

Opener	Responder
1 No Trump	2 Spades
2 No Trump	3 Spades

Opener MUST pass. This is the 100% sign-off.

Incidentally, there is no such bidding sequence as

South	North
1 No Trump	2 Spades
3 No Trump	

When you hear any such bidding sequence you will likely find opener is the possessor of an untutored brow. Either that, or he is quite sure that his partner is an unaware character, and that the affairs of state rest squarely on his own shoulders. In this sequence of bids, if the identity of the players is undetermined, the odds slightly favor South's being the husband.

Takeout to 3 of a Suit

Where responder's hand contains the high card values for a raise to 3 No Trump (that is, at least 10 points) and also contains a long suit, a jump in that suit may be given, e.g.,

Partner opens 1 No Trump. You hold:

♠ K Q x x x
♡ x
♢ A J x x
♣ x x x

Your hand contains the high card requirements for a jump to 3 No Trump, but a jump to 3 Spades is preferable.

Again partner opens 1 No Trump. You hold:

♠ x
♡ A J x x
◇ K Q x x x x
♣ x x

Respond with 3 Diamonds. This is the equivalent of contracting for game in No Trump, but it has one additional advantage: opener may have had a four card Heart suit at which the hand might play more conveniently, and the 3 Diamond bid will afford opener the chance to bid 3 Hearts. If he goes on to 3 No Trump, of course you relax.

Takeout to 4 of a Major

This is done with a hand containing a long suit (at least six cards) but less than 10 points in high cards. Responder should expect to win about five tricks in his own hand.

Partner opens 1 No Trump. You hold:

♠ K Q J 10 x x
♡ x
◇ x x
♣ 10 x x x

Respond 4 Spades, which opener must pass.

Responses to Opening Bids of 2 No Trump (With Balanced Hands)

Always add your points to those shown by partner's opening.

With 4 to 8 points raise to 3 No Trump. You know there

is no slam, since the most partner can have is 24 points
$(24 + 8 = 32)$.

With 9 points raise to 4 No Trump. There may be a slam,
if partner has a maximum of 24 points $(24 + 9 = 33)$.

With 10 points there will be a slam unless partner has a
minimum (22 points). Therefore, first bid a suit and then
raise to 4 No Trump. Bidding a suit and raising to 4 No
Trump is stronger than just bidding 4 No Trump.

With 11 or 12 points bid 6 No Trump. You have at least
33 points if partner has a minimum of 22 $(22 + 11 = 33)$
and at most you have 36 if partner has a maximum of 24
$(24 + 12 = 36)$.

With 13 or 14 points first bid a suit and then bid 6 No
Trump. This is stronger than just bidding 6 No Trump directly. It asks partner to bid 7 if he has a maximum.

With 15 points you may bid 7 No Trump. No checking
for Aces is necessary, for opponents cannot have one if partner has bid correctly $(22 + 15 = 37)$. Opponents have at
most 3 points.

(With Unbalanced Hands)

(1) Bid any six card major suit regardless of the high card
content of your hand.

(2) Bid any five card major suit if your hand contains at
least 4 points in high cards.
(This may be shaded to 3 points with a highly unbalanced hand.)

(3) Jump to 4 in a major suit with a six card suit and a
hand containing about 8 points in high cards.

(4) Do not show minor suits unless the hand has slam possibilities. Even with six card suits the No Trump should
be raised.

Examples:

Partner opens with 2 No Trump. You hold:

<table>
<tr><td colspan="2" align="center">(A)</td><td colspan="2" align="center">(B)</td></tr>
<tr><td>♠</td><td>K 10 x x x</td><td>♠</td><td>10 9 x x x x x</td></tr>
<tr><td>♡</td><td>Q x x</td><td>♡</td><td>x</td></tr>
<tr><td>◇</td><td>x</td><td>◇</td><td>x x x</td></tr>
<tr><td>♣</td><td>x x x x</td><td>♣</td><td>x x</td></tr>
<tr><td colspan="2" align="center">(C)</td><td colspan="2" align="center">(D)</td></tr>
<tr><td>♠</td><td>K Q 10 x x x</td><td>♠</td><td>K Q x x x</td></tr>
<tr><td>♡</td><td>x</td><td>♡</td><td>x x</td></tr>
<tr><td>◇</td><td>x x</td><td>◇</td><td>J x x</td></tr>
<tr><td>♣</td><td>K x x x</td><td>♣</td><td>K x x</td></tr>
</table>

(A) Bid 3 Spades. If partner rebids 3 No Trump or 4 Spades, pass. With only 5 points in high cards, no slam is to be visualized. But the hand may play better in Spades.

(B) Bid 3 Spades. If partner bids 3 No Trump, bid 4 Spades. This hand must play in Spades and you arrange to do so by bidding Spades one at a time at the cheapest posssible level. Do not make the mistake of jumping to 4 Spades.

(C) Bid 4 Spades. This shows a six card suit with enough high cards to produce a slam opposite a maximum 2 No Trump bid. You have 8 points in high cards. If partner has 24, you will have 32 which with a good six card suit will sometimes be enough for a slam.

(D) Bid 3 Spades, a one round force, intending to raise to 4 No Trump next round. You have 9 points in high cards. If partner has 24 it should be an easy slam.

Responses to Opening Bids of
3 No Trump

Remember partner has 25 to 27, keep your eye on the figures 33 (small slam) and 37 (grand slam).

With a five card suit and five points in high cards show that suit.

♠ K Q x x x
♡ x x x
◇ x x x
♣ x x

Bid 4 Spades.

With 7 points and no five card suit bid 4 No Trump.

With 8 or 9 points bid 6 No Trump. You have at least 33 and at most 36.

With 10 or 11 points bid 4 Diamonds,* and then rebid 6 No Trump on the next round. Partner should bid 7 with a maximum opening. Showing a suit and then bidding 6 No Trump is stronger than a direct leap to 6 No Trump.

With 12 points bid 7 No Trump. No checking for Aces is necessary. Opponents can't have one $(25+12=37)$.

---

*The Diamond bid is really artificial—4 of a major cannot be employed in this situation because opener may pass; and 4 Clubs is used as a conventional asking bid, (The Gerber Convention). See Chapter VII.

CHAPTER VI

Rebids by Opening
No Trump Bidder

THE OPENING No Trump bidder is not expected to take drastic action of his own volition. He has presumably told his whole story on the opening bid, and all display of heroism should be left to his partner. There is one thing he may not yet have told, i.e., whether his opening was minimum or maximum. In cases where it was maximum he may take forward action only *when coaxed to do so* by responder. That's why there is no such bidding as

Opener	Responder
1 No Trump	2 Hearts
3 No Trump	

There are several instances in which opener MUST pass.
(a) When responder bids 3 No Trump
(b) When responder bids 4 Hearts or 4 Spades
(c) When responder raises to 2 No Trump and opener has a minimum No Trump bid of 16 points
(d) When responder bids 2 of a suit and opener has a minimum of 16 points.

The Check Back for Major Suits

Frequently responder raises to 2 No Trump on a hand that contains a representative four card holding in Spades or Hearts. If there is a weak spot in the No Trump, it may well be that the major suit will offer a safer road to game if each partner holds four of the suit. It is fundamental tactics therefore that, whenever during the course of the bidding an opening No Trump bidder is on the verge of going to 3 No Trump, he might as well stop off on the way to try out a four card major suit, e.g.,

North—♠ x x   ♡ K x x x   ◇ Q J x x   ♣ K x x
South—♠ Q 10 x   ♡ Q J x x   ◇ A K x   ♣ A J x

South	North
1 No Trump	2 No Trump
3 Hearts	4 Hearts

South, the opener, has 17 points and calls 1 No Trump. North raises to 2 No Trump with 9 points. South "checks back" for a possible 4-4 major suit fit in Hearts. North having four Hearts and a weakness in Spades proceeds to game; and the correct final contract is reached.

Rebid by Opening No Trumper
When Responder Bids
2 Clubs or 2 Diamonds

Since responder is known to have less than 7 points, opener should not take further action unless his No Trump was about maximum (18 or 19).

Where opener has a near maximum No Trump, *which includes two high honors in responder's suit* (A-K-x, A-Q-x, or K-Q-x), he should raise to 3 of the minor. This bid responder is at liberty to pass, but occasionally responder will be in position to go on to 3 No Trump with a relatively weak hand, when he is assured that his six or seven card suit is established, e.g.,

North—♠ x   ♡ K x x   ◊ Q 10 x x x x   ♣ x x x
South—♠ Q J x   ♡ A x x   ◊ A K x   ♣ K J x x

South bids 1 No Trump. North responds 2 Diamonds, announcing an unbalanced hand that is weak in high cards. South, who has a near maximum No Trump including two of the top honors in Diamonds, raises to 3. North may pass if he chooses, but knowing that his partner has the Ace and King of Diamonds which will probably permit the cashing of six tricks in that suit, he may take a chance on 3 No Trump.

CHAPTER VII

The Gerber 4 Club Convention

Sometimes a grand slam can be made with a great many points less than the normal 37, when responder holds a very long suit.

In cases of that kind, of course, it will be desirable to check on Aces—since the opposition may have as many as 10 points. At such times the Gerber Convention (4 Clubs) will be useful.

Your partner opens 1 No Trump and you hold:

♠ x
♡ x x
♢ A K Q x x x x x
♣ A x

You know that you will play for at least 6 Diamonds but if partner has the key cards you can make a grand slam. It is possible that partner has a maximum No Trump but lacks one of the Aces. For example he might hold:

♠ K Q J
♡ A Q J
♢ J x x
♣ K Q x x

In order to determine this you burst into 4 Clubs (The Gerber Convention). This is a request for Aces. If part- ner shows two Aces and two Kings you may contract for 7 No Trump. Even if he shows two Aces and only one King you may, if you choose, take the reasonable risk that he has a Queen with one of his Kings and bid 7 anyhow.

A sudden burst from 1 or 2 No Trump to 4 Clubs is an artificial bid and is treated in the Blackwood manner as a request for Aces. The responses are:

4 Diamonds	—	No Aces
4 Hearts	—	1 Ace
4 Spades	—	2 Aces
4 No Trump	—	3 Aces
5 Clubs	—	4 Aces

The 4 Club bidder may then ask for Kings by calling the next legal bid above partner's response. If, in response to the 4 Club bid, opener bids 4 Hearts (indicating 1 Ace), the 4 Club bidder may bid 4 Spades (the next legal bid), which would be a request for Kings. The response of 4 No Trump would then show no Kings; 5 Clubs—one King; etc., etc.

Let us suppose in response to the 4 Club bid opener called 4 Spades (showing 2 Aces). If the 4 Club bidder wishes to ask for Kings he makes the next legal bid, which is 4 No Trump. Five Clubs would then show no Kings, etc.

IN BRIEF

26 points will normally produce game.

33 points will normally produce a small slam.

37 points will normally produce a grand slam.

Opening 1 No Trump—16 to 19 points
Opening 2 No Trump—22 to 24 points
Opening 3 No Trump—25 to 27 points

Responses to Opening 1 No Trump Bids:

Raise to 2 No Trump with 8 or 9 points (or 7 points with a five card suit)

Raise to 3 No Trump with 10 to 14 points

Raise to 4 No Trump with 15 or 16 points

Raise to 6 No Trump with 17 or 18 points

Bid 3 of a suit, then 6 No Trump with 19 or 20 points

Raise to 7 No Trump with 21 points

A response of 2 Clubs or 2 Diamonds shows less than 7 points

A response of 2 Hearts or 2 Spades may contain as many as 8 points, but shows a five card suit and an unbalanced hand

A response of 4 Spades or 4 Hearts shows a long suit (six or seven cards) with less than 10 points in high cards

A response of 3 in any suit shows a hand with 10 or more points and a good suit

Responses to 2 No Trump Bids:

Raise to 3 No Trump with 4 to 8 points

Raise to 4 No Trump with 9 points

Bid 3 of a suit, then 4 No Trump with 10 points

Raise to 6 No Trump with 11 or 12 points

Bid 3 of a suit, then 6 No Trump, with 13 or 14 points

Raise to 7 No Trump with 15 points

With a five card major suit headed by an honor, and 4
   points, bid that suit at the level of 3

Show any six card major suit

Don't bother to show minor suits unless you contemplate
   a slam

Responses to 3 No Trump Bids:

Raise to 4 No Trump with 7 points

Raise to 6 No Trump with 8 or 9 points

Bid 4 Diamonds, then 6 No Trump with 10 or 11 points

Raise to 7 No Trump with 12 points

Show any five card suit if the hand contains 5 points in
   high cards

CHAPTER VIII

A Few General Hints
on the Valuation Table

IT WILL BE observed that in all No Trump situations I have given precise limits, where one bid ends and another begins. Because the danger of duplication is minimized, such precision is possible. But in suit bidding I have made no pretense at this type of accuracy. You will note that the top limit of one bid is also considered the lower limit of the next bid, e.g., in valuing your hand for the purpose of responding to partner's opening bid of 1 in a suit, the following table is submitted:

6 -10 Mediocre hand (worth only one bid)
10-13 Fairly good hand (worth two bids)
13-16 Very good hand. Responder should insist upon game
16-19 Powerful hand, worth more than a mere game force
19 & up Slam zone. Jump shift is indicated.

You will see that hands counting 10, 13, 16, and 19 points may be placed in one category or the other. They are the JUDGMENT POINTS. That is to say, in these cases you use your own judgment. Put them in the upper bracket if you feel bullish; in the lower bracket if you feel bearish. In this respect I am not merely consulting your whims. There are various factors that may properly induce an optimistic or a pessimistic attitude. It is perhaps needless to say that the point count is not a substitute for thinking.

Nor has any pretense been made for the infallibility of the point count method. Just as the honor trick table has its imperfections, the point count has certain slight defects which I feel it my duty to point out to you. When a hand possesses certain flaws a deduction of 1 point should be made in the count.

A hand without an Ace is considered to possess a flaw in the case of the opening bidder.

♠ K Q x   (5)
♡ K Q x   (5)
◇ Q J x x x (3)
♣ x x   (1)

On the surface this hand counts 14 points and would therefore be a mandatory opening. However, the hand is Aceless, a flaw for which there should be 1 point deduction. So that this hand is not an obligatory opening, and you may exercise your option to pass.

A hand with less than two quick tricks is considered to possess a flaw, in the case of the opening bidder. The quick tricks are briefly:

A K   (2)
A Q   (1½)
A   (1)
K Q x   (1)
K x   (½)

Any hand that contains an insufficiently guarded honor is considered to possess a flaw. A doubleton Jack or a Queen, unaccompanied by another honor (Q x or J x), is obviously not as impressive as a Queen or a Jack in association with another face card (K Q x or Q J x). Now here is where your judgment comes in. Where part of your count is made up of scattered Jacks or Queens, and you have reached one of these judgment points, exercise your discretion by placing these hands in the lower bracket.

A recent publication quoted a heckler as confronting us with the following hand:

♠ Q J
♡ Q J 10 x x
♢ Q J x
♣ Q J x

Inasmuch as it counted 13 points he demanded that we open it, which we refused to do. In the first place, 13 points is only an optional opening. Secondly, this hand is not worth 13 points. It is Aceless, which calls for the deduction of 1 point. It possesses unguarded honors in Spades. Furthermore, it lacks the required two defensive tricks.

The following insufficiently guarded holdings should be viewed with suspicion unless partner has already bid the suit.

A J alone	K J alone
K Q alone	Q x
Q J alone	J x

When borderline situations present themselves, hands containing the above combinations had better be treated in the conservative manner. In other words, whenever these hands count up to one of the judgment points, it is well to place them in the lower bracket.

Bidding With a Part Score

When a part score is held a slight modification in tactics is indicated. But the basic principles remain unaltered.

With nothing on score, when responder names a new suit, opener is under compulsion to speak again. But when holding a part score, where responder's bid completes a game contract, opener is under no such obligation. Where opener is satisfied with responder's call, no good purpose can be served by continuing the bidding beyond the game level. Raises which carry the bidding beyond the game level are a direct slam invitation.

A jump shift, however, forces partner to speak again even when game has been reached. Since the showing of a new suit is not forcing when a part score is held, the requirements for a jump shift should be relaxed by a point or two whenever a player senses slam possibilities.

However, an opening bid of two in a suit is still a demand bid, even though contract for game is actually reached by such a call. Responder must reply once. *After that he is at liberty to retire from the bidding* unless opener jumps in a new suit; in which case he must bid once more. It is therefore permissible to open with a two demand bid with 1 or 2 points less than the standard requirements.

Possession of a part score will justify opening some hands that would normally be considered questionable openings (because of the inconvenience of a rebid.) But, inasmuch as a rebid will not be required if partner's response reaches a game contract, those hands may be opened safely.

For example:

♠ — A x x   ♡ — A K J x   ◊ — J x x   ♣ — x x x

This hand contains only 13 points and the option to open should not be exercised from a clear score because no convenient rebid would be available if partner responded with 2 Clubs or 2 Diamonds. But with a 60 part score this hand should be opened, because when partner responds with 2 Clubs or 2 Diamonds you are in position to pass.

CHAPTER IX

Responses to Bids of
One in a Suit

26 Points Will Normally Produce Game

THERE's nothing mysterious or arbitrary about this. For years I have been shouting the battle cry that AN OPEN-ING BID FACING AN OPENING BID WILL PRO-DUCE GAME. It is gratifying to report that the advice has been widely heeded.

Now you are offered the point count translation of this battle cry. Let us see how this operates. The normal mini-mum opening bid contains about 13 points; so that when an opening bid faces an opening bid the partnership pos-sesses about 26 points and should reach game if a conveni-ent contract can be found.

Responding with Weak Hands

With hands of moderate strength responder may do one of three things:

(a) *Bid 1 No Trump*

This shows a balanced hand containing at least 6 and at most 9 points in high cards. (For the purpose of this re-sponse, as elsewhere in No Trump bidding, do not allow points for distribution.) Do not make this response of 1 No Trump if you are able to make a cheaper bid of 1 in a suit. This response of 1 No Trump is not forcing. IT IS A LIMIT BID—ITS LIMIT IS 9 POINTS IN HIGH CARDS.

(b) *Give a single raise in the suit bid*

With support for partner's suit a single raise may be given on hands ranging from 6 to 10 points. This may occasionally be shaded down to 5. It will be observed that the single raise has a slightly wider range than the No Trump response. This response is not forcing. IT IS A LIMIT BID —ITS LIMIT IS 10 POINTS IN HIGH CARDS AND DISTRIBUTION.

(c) *Bid 1 in a new suit*

The minimum requirement for this is 6 points. For this purpose, since your response is in a suit, distributional points are counted.

Examples:

Partner bids 1 Heart. You hold:

> ♠ x x x
> ♡ x x
> ◇ Q x x x
> ♣ K x x x

Pass. Your hand contains only 5 points and therefore you have not sufficient values to bid 1 No Trump. For purposes of No Trump responses, the doubleton is not counted.

Partner bids 1 Heart. You hold:

> ♠ x x x
> ♡ x x
> ◇ Q x x
> ♣ K x x x x

Pass. You have only 5 points in high cards which is not enough for a 1 No Trump response.

Partner bids 1 Heart. You hold:

    ♠ x x x
    ♡ x x
    ◇ K x x x
    ♣ K x x x

Respond 1 No Trump; you have 6 points.

Partner bids 1 Heart. You hold:

    ♠ K x x x x
    ♡ x x
    ◇ x x x
    ♣ Q x x

Respond 1 Spade. Since you are making a suit response this hand is worth 6 points (5 in high cards and 1 for the doubleton). A one over one response may sometimes be shaded to 5 points including high cards and distribution.

The one over one response is not a limit bid. For, at its maximum, it may be a very powerful hand and one that is just short of a jump shift. Responder has chosen to play a waiting game. Responder assumes no risk of being dropped, for his bid is absolutely forcing for one round.

Opening bid is 1 Club. Responder holds:

(A)	(B)
♠ 10 x x x	♠ x x
♡ K Q x x	♡ A J x x x x
◇ x x x	◇ A Q x
♣ x x	♣ A x

In both cases the proper response is 1 Heart.

(A) This hand represents the minimum on which a one over one response should be made (5 points in high cards, and 1 point for the doubleton). If anyone in the audience responded 1 No Trump with this hand it is suggested that he wash out his mouth with soap and water.

(B) This hand is pretty nearly maximum. Its value is 17 points (15 points in high cards and 1 for each doubleton).

For Raises of Suit Bids

In raising partner's suit bid, one must compute the value of the hand (a) in high cards, (b) in short suits.

Naturally adequate trump support is presumed, since without normal trump support you will make some other bid in preference to raising your partner's suit.

(a) High cards are computed at their face value. However, one must have regard to the promoted value of a trump honor. Obviously the King of your partner's suit is worth more than a side King. It is a sure winner, and is the equivalent of an Ace. Similarly the Queen of partner's suit is worth more than a side Queen.

It has always been my practice to promote an honor in partner's suit to the next rank. The Ace, like the General, has no chance for advancement, and can be allotted no more than 4 points. The King of trumps, however, becomes promoted to the value of an Ace and counts 4 points; the Queen of trumps becomes promoted to the value of a King; the Jack of trumps becomes promoted to the value of a Queen.

The following are holdings in partner's suit which should be promoted:

$$K x x = 4$$
$$Q J x = 4$$
$$Q x x = 3$$
$$J \ x x = 2$$

However, if you have already counted at least 4 points in trumps, no promotion takes place.

The following combinations, therefore, all count at their exact face value; for you have already counted at least a full trick (4 points) in that suit, and no promotion takes place.

$$A K x = 7$$
$$A Q x = 6$$
$$A J \ x = 5$$
$$K Q x = 5$$
$$K J \ x = 4$$

(b) Short Suits:

    Add 1 point for each doubleton

    Add 3 points for each singleton

    Add 5 points for a void

(Note the difference in valuation of short suits between the opening bidder's hand and the responder's hand.)

Certain deductions are made when your hand, as prospective dummy, contains a flaw. There are three very common defects or flaws:

1. Possession of only three trumps when raising partner's suit is a flaw.

2. A 4-3-3-3 distribution is a flaw when raising partner's suit.

3. A short suit containing an insufficiently guarded honor is a flaw.

When dummy's hand is freakish, a strict adherence to point count requirements for a raise is not expected. If dummy contains five trumps, the requirements for a raise may be shaded by a point. For example, partner opens with 1 Spade and you hold:

♠ 10 x x x x   ♡ x x   ◇ K x x x   ♣ x x

This hand counts only 5 dummy points, but we would respond with a bid of 2 Spades. At least such action should serve as a partial pre-empt against fourth hand and in some cases may make it difficult for him to enter the auction.

However, let me point to an old slogan of mind: Don't let a fifth trump in dummy get you all excited.

Where dummy contains six trumps we have a freak situation, and delicacy of measurement cannot be achieved. In such cases your own instincts will generally serve as a reliable guide. In many cases a pre-emptive raise will be the best strategy despite a lack of point count. To point an extreme illustration, you are not vulnerable and your opponents are. Partner opens with 1 Spade. You hold:

♠ 10 x x x x x   ♡ x   ◇ Q x x   ♣ x x x

Unless partner has a powerhouse, opponents likely have a game. Some players would take a deliberate loss by pre-empting to 4 Spades. Occasionally such action might prove effective.

Responding with Strong Hands

(1) *The Jump Raise* (1 Spade—3 Spades)

This bid is forcing to game. Responder must have a little better than adequate trump support—at least four to an honor. The hand must contain 13 to 16 points. If your hand possesses the necessary point count, but lacks four trumps, you must temporize by naming a new suit and then support-ing partner next round.

Partner opens with 1 Spade. You hold:

(A)	(B)	(C)
♠ A 10 x x (4)	♠ K J x x (4)	♠ K 10 x x (4)†
♡ x (3)*	♡ A J x x (5)	♡ x x x
◇ x x x x	◇ x x (1)x	◇ A K x (7)
♣ A Q x x (6)	♣ A x x (4)	♣ K J x (4)
$\overline{13}$	$\overline{14}$	$\overline{15}$

* Note singleton in supporting hand is worth 3 points.
x Note doubleton in supporting hand is worth 1 point.
† Note King of trumps in supporting hand is promoted.

In each case respond 3 Spades. Hand (C) counts 15 points. Even with the 1 point deduction for the defect of the 4-3-3-3 distribution it is still worth 14 points and fully qualifies for a jump raise.

(2) *The Triple Raise* (1 Spade—4 Spades)

This bid describes a hand with a great deal of trump support (usually five), a singleton or a void, but *not more than 9 points in high cards*, e.g.,

Partner opens 1 Spade. You hold:

♠ A J x x x
♡ x x
◇ x
♣ K 10 x x x

Respond 4 Spades. This hand is worth 12 points (8 points in high cards, 3 for the singleton and 1 for the doubleton). It is not a complete "shut-out" bid. But partner must not expect to find more than 9 points in high cards.

(3) *The Jump Take-Out in No Trump* (1 Spade—2 No Trump)

This bid is forcing to game. Responder must have a balanced hand, with protection in all unbid suits and a point count of 13 to 15. The partnership is, therefore, assured of the necessary 26 points.

Partner opens with 1 Heart. You hold:

(A)		(B)	
♠ K J x	(4)	♠ A Q x	(6)
♡ x x	*	♡ x x x	
◇ A J x x	(5)	◇ A J x	(5)
♣ K J x x	(4)	♣ K J x x	(4)
	13		15

Respond 2 No Trump in both cases.

The Jump Take-out to 3 No Trump

This is a specialized bid that should be reserved for hands of the 4-3-3-3 distribution. With protection in all three unbid suits and a point count of 16 to 18, bid 3 No Trump.

Partner opens with 1 Spade. You hold:

(A)		(B)	
♠ J x x	(1)	♠ Q x x	(2)
♡ A Q x	(6)	♡ A J x	(5)
◇ A J x	(5)	◇ K Q 10 x	(5)
♣ K Q x x	(5)	♣ A K x	(7)
	17		19

(A) Respond 3 No Trump.

(B) This hand is too big for a 3 No Trump response. The proper call is a *jump shift* to 3 Diamonds. Unless partner has a very light opening this hand will produce a good play for a slam.

* Remember that distributional values are not counted in bidding No Trump.

The Jump Shift

This bid is absolutely forcing to game and strongly suggests slam possibilities. It should be made only when responder has a strong suit of his own or good support for partner's suit. Responder's point count should be at least 19.

Partner opens 1 Heart. You hold:

(A)		(B)	
♠ A K Q J x x	(10)	♠ x	(3)
♡ x	(2)	♡ K Q x x	(5)
◇ A Q x x	(6)	◇ A x x	(4)
♣ x x	(1)	♣ A K x x x	(7)
	19		19

With hand (A) a jump shift to 2 Spades is indicated. You have no support for partner, but have a self sustaining suit of your own. Since Spades are the contemplated trump you should value the hand as though you were the bidder. It has the value of 19 points, 16 in high cards, 2 for the singleton and 1 for the doubleton.

With hand (B) make a jump shift to 3 Clubs. Since Hearts are the contemplated trumps you should value your hand as a dummy. This, too, is worth 19 points, 16 in high cards and 3 for the singleton.

Responder Shows a New Suit at the Level of 2

This is a constructive bid and should be based on a fairly good hand. How good? Assuming your hand to be more or less evenly balanced you must not go into the 2 level with a new suit if your hand is an eligible 1 No Trump response. That is to say, if your *high card* values are no greater than 9 (exclusive of distribution), 1 No Trump is the proper response.

Where you have 10 points in high cards your hand is too good for 1 No Trump, and you must respond with a new suit, even if you must bid at the level of 2.

Partner opens 1 Spade. You hold:

	(A)			(B)	
♠	x x		♠	x x	
♡	Q x x	(2)	♡	x x x	
◇	K x x	(3)	◇	K Q x	(5)
♣	A x x x x	(4)	♣	A J x x x	(5)
		—			—
		9			10

(A) Respond 1 No Trump. You have 9 points in high cards, which makes it eligible for 1 No Trump. Therefore, this hand is not strong enough to bid 2 Clubs.

(B) Respond 2 Clubs. Your hand contains 10 points in high cards, which make it too big for a 1 No Trump response. Note that the hand is worth 11 points at Clubs, including 1 point for distribution.

1 No Trump Response
to a 1 Club Opening

(This is a specialized bid and should not be employed except in trained partnerships.)

Since a response of 1 No Trump normally shows a maximum of 9 points, and a 2 No Trump response a minimum of 13 points, when holding an in-between hand (containing

10, 11 or 12 points) responder must bid in a roundabout way, arranging to speak twice. The practice with these hands is frequently to bid a suit at the level of 2 (even if a suit must be manufactured for the purpose), and await partner's rebid before deciding on the second response.

However, when the opening bid is 1 Club, responder cannot very well respond with a new suit at the level of 2, since that would be a jump. Accordingly, many players have adopted the practice of using a 1 No Trump response to an opening Club bid in an exceptional manner. The 1 No Trump response to a Club bid denotes a hand possessing the following characteristics:

(1) A high card count of 10 or 11 points (a little short of a 2 No Trump response)

(2) An evenly balanced hand

(3) Potential stoppers in the other three suits

(4) No biddable major suit

A 1 No Trump response to a Club bid might, for example, be made on the following hand:

♠ K x x   (3)
♡ Q x x   (2)
◇ A 10 x x   (4)
♣ J x x   (1)

Opener should not pass this response if he has somewhat more than a minimum. If he had 15 points, or occasionally even 14 points, he should rebid to 2 No Trump. If he has 16 points he may rely on responder for 10, and is in a position to bid 3 No Trump himself. It should be observed that

C

this method of bidding does not embarrass responder when he holds less than 10 points opposite an opening Club bid. He may make a one over one response in any other suit or raise the Club suit. When this choice is presented, these players will frequently make a 1 Diamond response on a three card suit, permitting opener to bid again at the level of 1.

Responding with Adequate Trump Support

On hands containing adequate trump support for partner's major suit and a count of 6 to 10 points, it is sound policy to give partner a single raise in his suit in preference to showing your own suit. The reason is this:

Such hands are worth only one "forward going" bid. You cannot afford, with hands of this limited strength, to bid your own suit and also raise partner. The more important of the two choices (the raise of partner's major suit) should be selected.

This is another way of applying my RULE OF FOUR PLUS which I introduced some years ago. That rule provides that where a hand is worth four plus playing tricks in support of an opening bid it is too good for a single raise; and responder must first make a temporizing bid with the intention of supporting partner's suit on the next round. 10 points represent about four playing tricks, which is the top limit for a single raise. With hands that count 11 or a little more (i.e., four *plus* playing tricks) responder should arrange to bid twice, e.g.,

Partner opens with 1 Heart. Next hand passes. You hold:

(A)		(B)		(C)	
♠ x	(3)	♠ x x x		♠ x x x	
♡ A x x x	(4)	♡ A J x	(5)	♡ A J x	(5)
◇ Q x x x	(2)	◇ x x	(1)	◇ x x	(1)
♣ K 10 x x	(3)	♣ K J x x x	(4)	♣ K Q x x x	(5)
	12		10		11

(A) This hand is worth 12 points in support of Hearts. It is therefore, not quite strong enough for a jump to 3 Hearts, which would be forcing to game. However, it is too strong for a single raise, the top limit of which is 10; so you should arrange to bid twice. This you may accomplish by a temporizing bid of 2 Clubs. If partner rebids 2 Hearts, you raise to 3, showing 11 or 12 points.

(B) This hand appears to have the value of 10 points; but 1 point must be deducted for a holding of only three trumps, giving it a true value of 9. The hand is, therefore, worth only one forward bid and the proper call is 2 Hearts, not 2 Clubs.

(C) This hand is 1 point stronger than hand (B). Its true value is 10 points. This places it on the borderline between hands worth a single raise and those worth two bids. (A judgment point.) You may exercise your own judgment. My own preference would be in favor of aggressive action in this case; and I would arrange to bid twice by first calling 2 Clubs. The reason for the optimism is that all my values are clear cut. If one of my points were, let us say, the Jack of Spades or the Jack of Diamonds, I would feel less bullish and would exercise my judgment on the conservative side. I would in that case, respond merely 2 Hearts.

Responding After a Previous Pass

When a player has previously passed he must adopt a somewhat different attitude towards his responses. He must bear in mind that those responses are now no longer forcing (except a jump in a new suit). The mere naming of a new suit does not force his partner to speak again, nor does a jump raise, nor a jump in No Trump.

Responder must therefore be prepared to play the hand at whatever bid he happens to make. There is no longer available to him the temporizing bid. It follows, too, that since his bids are not forcing and since for all practical purposes he has denied possession of 13 points by his original pass, he may now jump with less than the normally required 13 points.

The jump response of 2 No Trump may now be made with 11 or 12 points instead of 13.

Similarly responder may raise from 1 Spade to 3 Spades with a little less than the required 13, e.g., as South you hold:

♠ K x x x
♡ K x x
♢ x x
♣ A x x x

The bidding has proceeded:

South	West	North	East
Pass	Pass	1 Spade	Pass
?			

What do you bid now?

If you had not previously passed, a temporizing bid would be in order. For this hand is too good for a single raise (its value is above 10 points) and not good enough for a forcing jump raise (its value is less than 13 points). The value of this hand for the purpose of raising Spades is 12 points, 4 for the King of Spades (promoted), 3 for the King of Hearts, 1 for the doubleton, and 4 for the Ace of Clubs.

If you had not previously passed, you would have arranged to make two bids. First a temporizing bid of 2 Clubs (forcing for one round) and then a raise of Spades on the next round.

Now you are at perfect liberty to respond 3 Spades. Partner will not expect you to have 13 points since you have already passed. If he has a shaded third hand opening he need not go on.

It would be improper for you to respond 2 Clubs, for partner might pass. Occasionally you will hold a passed hand which contains 13 points (or even more when valued in support of partner). In such cases you may raise directly to 4 Hearts or 4 Spades.

Similarly, as South you hold:

♠ x x
♡ K J x
♢ A J x x
♣ K x x x

The bidding has proceeded:

South	West	North	East
Pass	Pass	1 Spade	Pass
?			

What do you bid now?

If you had not previously passed you would temporize by bidding 2 Diamonds, a one round force. The hand is too strong for a 1 No Trump response (it has more than 9 points in high cards) and it is too weak for a game forcing response of 2 No Trump (it has less than 13 points in high cards).

Now, having 12 points, you may respond with 2 No Trump which is no longer forcing. If partner does not have more than 13 he need not go on.

Similarly a two over one response may be made with a little less after a previous pass.

As South you hold:

♠ x x
♡ x x x
♢ K x x
♣ A J x x x

The bidding has proceeded:

South	West	North	East
Pass	Pass	1 Spade	Pass
?			

What do you bid now?

If you had not previously passed it would be improper to respond 2 Clubs. Your hand would not be good enough to force partner to rebid at the level of 2. The proper response would have been 1 No Trump. (The hand contains only 8 points in high cards.) But now you may respond 2 Clubs because your bid is not forcing and partner need not go on.

CHAPTER X

Free Bids

ALL FREE BIDS must be based upon fairly good hands. When your right hand opponent has entered the auction, your partner automatically receives another chance to bid. It is, therefore, not necessary for you to strain a point to keep the bidding open with doubtful holdings.

Free Bid of 1 No Trump

A free bid of 1 No Trump describes a hand that is just a little better than an ordinary negative 1 No Trump response (the top limit of which is 9), but not quite as good as a 2 No Trump response (the lower limit of which is 13). In other words, a free bid of 1 No Trump describes a hand with 10, 11, or 12 points.

As South you hold:

(A)	(B)
♠ K 10 x	♠ K 10 x
♡ x x x	♡ x x x
◇ A x x	◇ A Q x
♣ J x x x	♣ J x x x

The bidding has proceeded:

North	East	South
1 Heart	1 Spade	?

With (A) you should pass. Do not bid 1 No Trump merely for the purpose of showing the Spade stopper. You have only 8 points. If East had passed you would, of course, be expected to respond with 1 No Trump.

Wtih (B) you should call 1 No Trump. You have 10 points and a stopper in the adverse suit.

The Single Raise as a Free Bid

A raise for the purpose of keeping the bidding open may be made with as little as 6 points. But when your right hand opponent inserts a bid, you should not make a free bid raise with less than 8 points (6 and 7 represent a weak raise; 8 and 9 represent a fairly good raise). On the other hand, a free single raise may be made with as many as 12 points (just a shade below a double raise).

As South you hold:

(A)	(B)
♠ x x	♠ x x
♡ Q x x x	♡ Q x x x
◇ x x x	◇ x x x
♣ A x x x	♣ K x x x

The bidding has proceeded:

North	East	South
1 Heart	1 Spade	?

With (A) bid 2 Hearts; your hand has the value of 8 points—3 for the Queen of Hearts (promoted), 4 for the Ace, and 1 for the doubleton.

With (B) pass. You would have raised to 2 Hearts had East passed. But this hand is not good enough for a free raise inasmuch as it counts but 7 points.

The One Over One as a Free Bid

Even at the level of 1 a free bid should denote a fairly good hand and therefore should not be made with less than 9 or 10 points.

When your free bid of a new suit must be made at the level of 2, slightly more strength will be expected of you.

As South you hold:

	(A)			(B)	
♠	A x x	(4)	♠	x x x x	
♡	K J x x x	(4)	♡	K Q x x	(5)
◇	x x	(1)	◇	x x	(1)
♣	x x x		♣	A x x	(4)
		9			10

The bidding has proceeded:

North	East	South
1 Club	1 Diamond	?

In both cases you may make a free bid of 1 Heart. In (A) you have 9 points, in (B) 10 points.

But if you hold:

♠	x x	(1)
♡	x x x	
◇	A K J x x	(8)
♣	x x x	
		9

And the bidding has proceeded:

North	East	South
1 Spade	2 Clubs	?

You should not make a free bid of 2 Diamonds. A free bid of a new suit at the level of 2 requires about 11 points.

But if your free bid at the level of 2 must be made in a suit that is higher in rank than your partner's, so that the bidding will naturally be jammed up to a high level, you will need about 12 or 13 points, about the equivalent of an opening bid. The same requirements apply if your first response must be made at the level of 3, i.e.

As South you hold:

♠ A K x x x (7)
♡ Q x x   (2)
♢ x x   (1)
♣ x x x

The bidding has proceeded:

North	East	South
1 Diamond	2 Clubs	?

Do not bid 2 Spades. This hand has the value of 10 points and is not strong enough to project the bidding to the level of 3, which a free bid of 2 Spades would do.

Change the holding slightly:

♠ x x x
♡ A K x x x
♢ Q J x
♣ x x

The bidding has proceeded:

North	East	South
1 Spade	2 Clubs	?

You may bid 2 Hearts with 11 points, for the bidding will not be forced into the 3 level by such action.

CHAPTER XI

Responses to Two Bids

THE METHOD I employ myself, and which I heartily recommend to you, is the simplest, the soundest, and the one that has proven the most effective throughout the years. It is not spectacular; it is not dramatic; but it is natural and logical and imposes no additional burden on what by now may be your overtaxed memory.

The negative response remains, as always, 2 No Trump. But where specific values are held the practice is this:

FIRST MAKE A NATURAL RESPONSE. THEN, WHEN THE TRUMP SUIT HAS BEEN ESTABLISHED, THE PARTNERSHIP SHOWS EACH ACE AND EACH KING INDIVIDUALLY.

The natural response may take the form of a simple raise (the most preferable response when adequate trump support is held) or a simple suit take-out, or a response of 3 No Trump. The minimum requirement in each case is 7 points, including one quick trick, or 8 points including one-half a quick trick.

Don't lose sight of the fact that responder may have:

(a) trump support, or

(b) a good suit of his own, or

(c) Aces and Kings.

All three factors are of vital importance, and perhaps they rank in the order I have stated them. In a pinch good card reading may permit you to make a fairly good stab at whether your partner has a certain Ace or King, but you can hardly be expected to guess that your partner has trump support for you, or that he has a good five card suit.

Let us examine a few illustrations.

	Opener		Responder
♠	A K x	♠	Q J 10 x x
♡	A K Q J 10 x	♡	x x x
◇	A x	◇	x x
♣	x x	♣	A x x

The bidding:

Opener	Responder
2 Hearts	2 Spades (1)
3 Hearts (2)	4 Clubs (3)
7 Hearts or	
7 No Trump (4)	

(1) In partnership language, "I have a hand containing at least 7 points including one quick trick and a five card suit headed by at least the Q-J."

(2) "The Heart suit is self sustaining and you may consider that I have fixed it as the established trump. Start showing your Aces."

(3) "I have the Ace of Clubs."

(4) "That's all I wanted to know. I can count thirteen tricks because I know you have a five card Spade suit and we have six Hearts, five Spades and two Aces. I was glad to hear about your Spade suit, for the Ace of Clubs alone would bring the total of tricks only up to ten."

Another example:

Opener	Responder
♠ A K Q x x	♠ J 9 x x
♡ K Q J x	♡ A x x
◇ A Q J x	◇ K x
♣ None	♣ x x x x

The bidding:

Opener	Responder
2 Spades	3 Spades (1)
4 Diamonds (2)	4 Hearts (3)
5 Hearts (4)	6 Diamonds (5)
7 Spades (6)	

(1) "I have trump support for you, at least 7 points with one quick trick, and shall tell you about Aces on the next round."

(2) "I have the Ace of Diamonds. Keep talking."

(3) "I have the Ace of Hearts, in case you are interested."

(4) "Charmed! I have the King of Hearts. What else have you to tell me?"

(5) "I'm sure you're interested in the King of Diamonds."

(6) "It's a pleasure to do business with you. Some fellows would have had the Ace of Clubs instead of the Ace of Hearts, or the King of Clubs instead of the King of Diamonds. I'm spreading this hand for a grand slam and hope that the 'sucker' on my left, with the Ace of Clubs, decides to double me."

Another example:

Opener	Responder
♠ A K	♠ x x
♡ A K 10 x x x x	♡ Q 9 x
◇ A x	◇ K x x x
♣ x x	♣ A x x x

The bidding:

Opener	Responder
2 Hearts	3 Hearts (1)
3 Spades (2)	4 Clubs (3)
4 Diamonds (4)	5 Diamonds (5)
6 No Trump (6)	

(1) "Normal trump support with at least 7 points including one quick trick. Start the description."

(2) "I have the Ace of Spades."

(3) "I have the Ace of Clubs."

(4) "I have the Ace of Diamonds."

(5) "I have the King of Diamonds."

(6) "I can count twelve top card tricks on the basis of the three things you have told me. (The one I appreciate the most was the Heart support)."

Incidentally at this point opener could temporize still further by bidding 5 Spades, showing the King. This would afford responder the chance to bid 6 Clubs if he had the King of Clubs, or conceivably 6 Diamonds if he had the Queen.

It will be observed that the first mention of a suit, after

trump has been fixed, shows the Ace. After the Ace has been shown, the next mention of that suit shows the King. After the Ace and King of a suit have been shown there will rarely be room for any further conversation, but if there should chance to be there is no reason why the third mention of the suit should not designate the Queen.

Ace Showing Over Two Bids

"Do you show Aces over two bids?" is a question you will be confronted with on many occasions. Some players, in response to an opening two bid, make it a practice to show Aces and Kings wholesale and without regard to the rest of the hand. They proceed upon the theory that the opening bidder's first named suit will be the final trump and that the suit is self sustaining. This is an entirely improper assumption. Their convention is a flashback to the old Sims' Three Bid, which in those days was used to designate a hand of the same strength as an opening two bid, except that the trump suit was absolutely solid and the only thing opening bidder lacked was Aces. It was a convention devised for freak hands; and it is not soundly applicable to our type of two demand bid, which may be based on a two suiter, or a suit that requires some support.

I believe in freedom of movement. I do not choose to have myself restricted to the showing of Aces and Kings only, when for no extra fee I may tell my partner whether I have support for his trumps or a suit of my own. Then I can show all the Aces and Kings I'm fortunate enough to hold, on later rounds.

In a word, when there is a choice between a natural and an artificial method, you are safe in wagering that over the course of time the natural method will prove superior.

I'm old fashioned enough to be interested in whether my partner has trump support for me. Many a two bid lacks the Queen of trumps. It's comforting to learn that partner has it.

Take the hand of page 13:

> ♠ A K J x x
> ♡ A
> ◇ A K x
> ♣ K Q 10 x

You open with 2 Spades. If partner holds hand (A) below a splendid play for slam is offered, despite the fact that it is Aceless. So responder, whose hand is worth 9 points in support of Spades, gives an immediate raise. Whereas hand (B), containing an Ace, presents virtually no play for slam.

(A)	(B)
♠ Q x x x	♠ x x
♡ K x x x x	♡ x x x x
◇ x x x	◇ x x x x
♣ x	♣ A x x

IN BRIEF

In making No Trump responses only the high card values are counted.

————

In making suit responses you may add the distributional points to your high card values.

————

In raising partner's suit bid you must employ the table of valuation for dummy hand, as follows:

    (A) Count high cards at face value

    (B) Promote honors in partner's suit

    (C) Add 1 point for a doubleton

                3 points for a singleton

                5 points for a void

Deduct 1 point if your hand contains only three trumps.

Deduct 1 point if your hand is distributed 4-3-3-3.

————

Respond 1 No Trump	6- 9 points
Respond 2 No Trump	13-15 points
Respond 3 No Trump	16-18 points

————

Raise partner's suit bid to 2	6-10 points
Raise partner's suit bid to 3	13-16 points
Make a jump shift	19 points

Show a new suit at 1 level   6 points

Show a new suit at 2 level   10 points

With hands counting 11 or 12 points find two bids without forcing partner to game.

CHAPTER XII

Rebids by Opener

Judging the Strength of My Hand As Opener

POINT COUNT
(13 to 16)

MY HAND IS IN THE MINIMUM RANGE. If I don't feel like it I shall not bid again unless my partner's response is forcing. If he gives me a single raise I shall pass. If he responds with 1 No Trump I shall pass unless my hand is unbalanced. If he names a new suit I shall be obliged to bid again, but I shall rebid at the most convenient level. My rebid will be 1 No Trump, or a repetition of my original suit, or some other suit that I can show cheaply. Or I may have to give partner a single raise.

(16 to 19)

I HAVE A GOOD HAND and I am in a position to make a constructive rebid. I shall avoid making any rebid which my partner may construe as discouraging.

(19 to 21)

I HAVE A VERY GOOD HAND. This is in the jump rebid range. I will either jump in No Trump, or jump in my own suit or in partner's suit. Unless something was wrong with partner's response, we will surely have game.

(22 and up)

> *THIS IS A SUPER HAND. Of course, we are going to game. I'll personally see to that by making a jump shift, which partner is not permitted to pass and which is forcing to game. If partner has a good hand we will have a slam.*

When responder raises the opening bid from 1 to 2, opener must revalue his hand. In making his original bid the opening bidder counted his high cards, together with his distributional values. He added 1 point for a doubleton and 2 points for a singleton and 3 points for a void. That was another way of saying that the fifth card of the trump suit was valued at 1 point, and so was the sixth card. In other words a suit like this: A K x x x—was valued at 8 points; and this: A K x x x x—was valued at 9 points.

That was a reasonable enough valuation at the time he picked his hand up, and before he knew that a fit would be established. But when partner raises, his hand undergoes a transformation. That doubtful five or six card suit now becomes solidified and the long cards are worth considerably more than they were before. This adjustment is made in the following manner:

WHEN PARTNER RAISES YOUR SUIT, ADD AN ADDITIONAL POINT FOR THE FIFTH TRUMP AND 2 ADDITIONAL POINTS FOR THE SIXTH, AND EACH SUBSEQUENT TRUMP.

I'm sorry to have to burden your memory with this one, but it's indispensable if you want to value your hand properly. If this adjustment is not made, here is what you are apt to be confronted with: you open 1 Spade and partner raises to 2; you hold:

♠ A K Q x x x
♡ A Q x
◇ x x x
♣ x

This hand has an original valuation of 17 points (15 in high cards and 2 for distribution). Since partner's raise may be based on as little as 6 points, you might not feel warranted in contracting for game. However you test him out by bidding only 3 and coaxing him to go forward. The poor unfortunate character, however, has raised on this colorless holding:

♠ x x x x
♡ x x
◇ K Q x x
♣ x x x

He has just 6 points, and quickly drops you at the 3 level. Here you are—playing for part score, though you are an outstanding favorite to go game.

What's wrong? You didn't revalue your hand after the raise. Add another point for the fifth trump and 2 points for the sixth, and your real valuation is now 20. Since partner has promised 6 points there's nothing more to wait for. You utter the words "Four Spades," and proceed with the relatively easy business of fulfilling your contract.

We apologize for adding this to the long string of figures you must commit to memory, but there is this bit of news that will be relished by the tired businessman: We have no more tables of values to offer you.

Raising Responder from 1 to 2
(14-15-16 POINTS)

Where opener has support for responder's major suit, he may raise from 1 to 2 with very little more *than a minimum* opening. Opener now revalues his hand as though it were a dummy for his partner; and if he has a little more than 13, which is the normal minimum opening, he may raise. A raise should not be made with less than 14 (1 point over the minimum), except when four trumps are held.

You open 1 Club. Partner responds 1 Spade. You hold:

(A) ♠ A x x	♡ x	◇ x x x x	♣ A K J x x (14)*
(B) ♠ A x x x	♡ x x	◇ J 10 x	♣ A K J x (14)*
(C) ♠ A x x	♡ x x	◇ J x x	♣ A K J x x (13)*

With hands (A) and (B) raise to 2 Spades. They each have 14 points (a little over minimum) with trump support for partner. With hand (C) rebid 2 Clubs. This is an absolute minimum, and the raise should not be given.

Raising Responder from 1 to 3
(17 TO 19 POINTS)

You open 1 Club. Partner responds 1 Spade. You hold:

♠ A x x x (4)
♡ K Q x x (5)
◇ x (3)
♣ A Q x x (6)

Bid 3 Spades. Your hand has a value of 18 points in support of Spades.

*These hands are all revalued as in support of a Spade bid by partner.

You open 1 Diamond. Partner responds 1 Spade. You hold:

> ♠ A x x x   (4)
> ♡ K x   (4)
>   (3 for King; 1 for doubleton)
> ♦ A K J x x (8)
> ♣ x x   (1)

Bid 3 Spades. Your hand has a value of 17 points in support of Spades. This bid is not forcing. Responder may exercise his option to pass if his response was based on 6 or 7 points. However, if his response contained 8 or 9 points, he must go on.

Raising Responder from 1 to 4

(19 TO 21 POINTS)

You open 1 Club. Partner responds 1 Spade. You hold:

> ♠ K Q x x   (5)
> ♡ A J x x   (5)
> ♦ x   (3)
> ♣ A K J x   (8)

Bid 4 Spades. Your hand has the value of 21 points in support of Spades.

You open 1 Club. Partner responds 1 Spade. You hold:

> ♠ K Q x x   (5)
> ♡ A x x   (4)
> ♦ x   (3)
> ♣ A K x x x (7)

Bid 4 Spades. This hand has the value of 19 points in support of Spades. This bid is by no means a shut out; and if partner has 11 or 12 points he should show some animation. Let us have none of this Gay Nineties chatter—"Partner, you jumped to game, that shut me out!"

Jump Rebid to 2 No Trump

(19 AND 20 POINTS)

♠ x x
♡ K Q x   (5)
◇ A K J x   (8)
♣ A Q x x   (6)

You open 1 Diamond. Partner responds 1 Spade. You have 19 points in high cards. It will take about 7 in partner's hand to reach the required 26; but he may not have that many. He may have as little as 5 in high cards (plus perhaps another point for distribution). You are therefore not in position to contract for game. You should jump to 2 No Trump. If partner has 7 he must go on to game. Even if he has only 6 points in high cards, he'll probably take a chance.

Jump Rebid to 3 No Trump

(21 AND 22 POINTS)

♠ 10 x
♡ A Q x   (6)
◇ A K J x   (8)
♣ A Q J x   (7)

You open 1 Diamond. Partner responds 1 Spade. You have 21 points in high cards. Even if partner has a shaded response you will have the required 26. Bid 3 No Trump.

Jump Rebid in Opener's Own Suit
(16 TO 19 POINTS)

This may be done provided opener has a solid five-card suit or a very good six-card suit.

♠ x x   (1)
♥ A K 10 x x x (7)
♦ A Q x   (6)
♣ K x   (4)

(3 for King; 1 for doubleton)

Rebid 3 Hearts. Your hand is worth 18 points and contains a good six-card suit.

Jump Shift by Opener
(22 POINTS AND UP)

You open 1 Club. Partner responds 1 Spade. You hold:

♠ K x x x   (4)
♥ x   (3)
♦ A K x   (7)
♣ A K Q x x (9)

Bid 3 Diamonds. (A manufactured jump shift.) Your hand is worth 23 points in support of Spades and is too big for a raise to 4 Spades. The immediate slam signal should be flashed.

Rebid by Opener When Responder Bids 2 of a New Suit

Whenever opening bidder on his rebid makes it impossible for responder to return to 2 of the first suit, he announces a strong hand (somewhere between 16 and 19 points), e.g.,

	Opener	Responder
(a)	1 Heart	2 Diamonds
	2 No Trump	?
(b)	1 Heart	2 Diamonds
	3 Diamonds	?
(c)	1 Heart	2 Diamonds
	3 Clubs	?
(d)	1 Heart	2 Diamonds
	2 Spades	?
(e)	1 Spade	2 Hearts
	3 Hearts	

In each of these cases responder finds it impossible to return to 2 Hearts. Opener has therefore promised a strong hand:

(a) at least 16 points in high cards

(b) at least 16 points in support

(c) at least 19 rebid points

(d) at least 19 rebid points

(e) this raise may be given with 15 points, or even a point less, where four of partner's trumps are held. In this respect it differs from a raise to 3 of a minor suit which requires at least 16 points.

Examples of Rebids by Opener

You are South in the following hands. The bidding has proceeded:

	South		North
	1 Spade		1 No Trump
	?		

What do you bid now?

	(A)			(B)	
♠	A K J x x	(8)	♠	A K x x	(7)
♡	x x		♡	A Q x x	(6)
◇	K J x	(4)	◇	x x x	
♣	J x x	(1)	♣	x x	

	(C)			(D)	
♠	A K x x	(7)	♠	A K 10 x	(7)
♡	A Q x	(6)	♡	A Q x	(6)
◇	A 10 x x	(4)	◇	A x x x	(4)
♣	J x	(1)	♣	K J	(4)

(A) Pass. You have only 13 points in high cards. Even if partner has the maximum of 9, you will have no game. Your hand is balanced, and Spades should not be rebid.

(B) Pass. You have only 13 points in high cards, so there is no possible game. Your hand is balanced, so your second suit should not be shown.

(C) Bid 2 No Trump, which in this sequence requires 18 or 19 points. If partner's No Trump is on the lower side (6 points) there will be no game and he will pass but if it is on the upper side (8 or 9 points) he should go on to 3 No Trump. With 7 points he may exercise his own judgment.

(D) Bid 3 No Trump. You have 21 points in high cards. Even if Partner has a minimum No Trump of only 6 points you will have enough.

You are South in the following hands. The bidding has proceeded:

South	North
1 Spade	2 Spades
?	

What do you bid now?

(A)		(B)	
♠ A K x x x	(7)	♠ A K x x x	(7)
♡ A x x	(4)	♡ A J x	(5)
◊ Q x x	(2)	◊ K J x	(4)
♣ x x	(1)	♣ x x	(1)

(C)	
♠ A K x x	(7)
♡ x x x	
◊ A Q 10 x	(6)
♣ A x	(5)

(A) Pass. Your hand has an original valuation of 14 points. Adding a point for the fifth card of your supported trump suit brings it up to 15 points. Even if partner has the maximum of 10, you will be slightly short of game.

(B) Bid 3 Spades. Your hand has an original valuation of

17 points. Adding a point for the fifth card of your supported trump suit brings the value to 18. If partner's raise was on the lower side (6 or 7 points) you will not have quite enough and he should pass, but if it is on the upper side (8 or 9 points) he should go on to 4 Spades.

(C) Bid 3 Diamonds. Your hand has a value of 18 points. If partner's raise was based on 6 points there will probably be no game, but if it is based on 8 or 9 points there will be. The 3 Diamond bid asks him to go to game if his raise was in the upper bracket. He must then bid either 4 Spades or 3 No Trump. If he returns to 3 Spades it will mean that he had a light raise and you should quit.

As South you hold:

$$\spadesuit \ A \ K \ x \ x \ x \ (7)$$
$$\heartsuit \ x \ x \qquad (1)$$
$$\diamondsuit \ K \ J \ x \qquad (4)$$
$$\clubsuit \ A \ x \ x \qquad (4)$$

The bidding has proceeded:

South	North
1 Spade	3 Spades
?	

Your hand had an original valuation of 16 points. Adding a point for the fifth card of your supported trump suit, your hand is worth 17 points. North's hand ranges from 13 to 16 points. If it is maximum you may have a slam. Suggest it by bidding 4 Clubs, showing the Ace. If partner merely returns to 4 Spades, you will have done your duty and should retire. If partner bids 4 Diamonds—you may carry on by bidding 5 Diamonds, showing the King. The rest will be up to him.

As South you hold:

$$
\begin{array}{lll}
\spadesuit & A\ K\ x\ x\ x & (7) \\
\heartsuit & x\ x & (1) \\
\diamondsuit & A\ Q\ x & (6) \\
\clubsuit & K\ Q\ x & (5)
\end{array}
$$

The bidding has proceeded:

South	North
1 Spade	3 Spades
?	

Your hand had an original valuation of 19. Adding a point for the fifth card of your supported trump suit, your hand is worth 20 points. So, even if partner has a minimum of 13, you will have enough for a slam; and you may sit right up in your chair and bid 6 Spades. or you may get a little more mileage out of this hand by first bidding 4 Diamonds.

CHAPTER XIII

Rebids By Responder

Judging the Strength of My Hand As Responder

POINT COUNT
(6 to 10)

> MY HAND IS IN THE MINIMUM
> RANGE AND I SHALL MAKE A MILD
> RESPONSE. *However, I may act again if
> partner coaxes me to. If I have only 6 points
> I won't be coaxed to take further action. But
> if I have 8 or 9 points, and partner invites me
> to speak again, I shall do so cheerfully. With
> 7 points I shall use my own judgment.*

(10 to 13)

> I HAVE A GOOD HAND. *It is worth two
> bids; and to be sure that I get two chances I
> shall make a response which opener is not per-
> mitted to pass. That is, I will temporarily bid
> a new suit.*

(13 to 16)

> I HAVE A VERY GOOD HAND AND
> MUST SEE TO IT THAT WE REACH
> GAME; *for I have an OPENING BID FAC-
> ING AN OPENING BID. That is to say, our
> partnership has at least 26 points. I shall,
> therefore, either make an immediate game*

> forcing bid, or keep making bids which open-
> er may not pass (new suits) until we reach a
> satisfactory game contract.

(16 to 19)

> *I HAVE A VERY POWERFUL HAND. A*
> *mere game demand response would not be*
> *sufficient. I must show that I have more than*
> *an opening bid. I may do this by jumping to*
> *3 No Trump (instead of 2 No Trump), or by*
> *bidding a suit and then making a big jump the*
> *next round.*

(19 and up)

> *THIS HAND WILL PRODUCE A SLAM*
> *UNLESS PARTNER HAS A MINIMUM.*
> *I must, therefore, give the immediate slam*
> *signal by jumping in a new suit. The Jump*
> *Shift.*

Examples of Rebids by Responder

You are South in the following hands. The bidding has
proceeded:

North	South
1 Spade	1 No Trump
2 No Trump	?

What do you bid now?

	(A)			(B)	
♠	x x		♠	x x	
♡	Q x x	(2)	♡	K x x x	(3)
◊	K J x x	(4)	◊	Q x x	(2)
♣	Q x x x	(2)	♣	Q x x x	(2)

(A) Bid 3 No Trump. Your response contained 8 points in high cards; it was therefore in the upper bracket (it might have been only 6 or 7) and you should accept partner's invitation to proceed.

(B) Pass. Your hand has only 7 points and is in the lower side of the No Trump response. You should decline the invitation.

———

You are South in the following hands. The bidding has proceeded:

North	South
1 Spade	2 Spades
3 Spades	?

What do you bid now?

	(A)			(B)	
♠	Q x x x	(3)	♠	Q x x x	(3)
♡	x x	(1)	♡	x x	(1)
◊	Q x x x	(2)	◊	K x x x	(3)
♣	A x x	(4)	♣	x x x	

(A) Bid 4 Spades. Your hand is worth 10 points, which makes it a maximum raise. (Note the Queen of trumps is promoted to the value of a King.)

(B) Pass. Your hand is worth only 7 points, which places it in the lower bracket, and you should decline the invitation.

As South you hold:

    ♠ J x x   (1)
    ♡ A K x x   (7)
    ◇ K x x x   (3)
    ♣ x x

The bidding has proceeded:

North	South
1 Club	1 Heart
1 No Trump	?

Don't give up the ship. You have 11 points in high cards and it is your duty to speak twice. Raise to 2 No Trump. Partner may have 15 points, in which case he will carry on.

As South you hold:

    ♠ x x x
    ♡ A 10 x x x   (4)
    ◇ x x   (1)
    ♣ A x x   (4)

The bidding has proceeded:

North	South
1 Diamond	1 Heart
2 Diamonds	?

Pass. Your hand has the value of only 9 points (including the point for distribution) and you are entitled to only one bid. Partner cannot have as many as 17 points else he would have made an encouraging rebid.

As South you hold the following hands:

(A)			(B)		
♠ x x			♠ x x		
♡ A K x x x	(7)		♡ A K x x x	(7)	
◊ Q J x	(3)		◊ J x x	(1)	
♣ K J x	(4)		♣ K J x	(4)	

(C)			(D)		
♠ J x x	(1)		♠ J x x	(1)	
♡ A K x x x	(7)		♡ A K x x x	(7)	
◊ x x	(1)		◊ x x	(1)	
♣ K J x	(4)		♣ Q x x	(2)	

The bidding has proceeded:

North	South
1 Spade	2 Hearts
2 Spades	?

(A) Your hand is well adapted to No Trump play and you have a high card point count of 14. Even if partner has a minimum you will have enough and your proper bid is 3 No Trump.

(B) Since partner has not supported Hearts and you cannot support Spades an effort should be made to reach a No Trump game. You cannot quite reach it yourself, for you have only 12 points and you have not complete protection in Diamonds, but you should move in

that direction by bidding 2 No Trump, which partner
will pass only if he has opened a minimum hand. If he
has 14, he should go to 3.

(C) Bid 4 Spades. You have normal trump support for a
rebid suit and your hand has the value of 13 points in
support of Spades. (Remember the Jack of Spades is
promoted but there is a deduction for only three
trumps.) The partnership, therefore, presumably has
26 points.

(D) Bid 3 Spades. Your hand is worth only 11 points in
support of Spades and partner must be given a chance
to pass if he has a minimum. (Remember there is a
deduction of 1 point for only three trumps.)

———

As South you hold:

♠ x x   (1)
♥ A K 10 x x (7) + 1 rebid point
♦ x x x
♣ Q x x   (2)

The bidding has proceeded:

North	South
1 Diamond	1 Heart
2 Hearts	?

Your hand had an original value of 10 points; adding 1
point for the fifth card of the supported Heart suit brings
the total to 11. Partner's hand is known to range from 14 to
16. If it happens to be 15 or 16, you will have enough. You
should, therefore, coax partner to go on by bidding 3 Hearts.

♠ x x   (1)
♡ A K 10 x x (7) + 1 rebid point
♢ x x x
♣ K J x   (4)

The bidding has proceeded as above. You should bid 4 Hearts. Your hand has a rebid value of 13 points. Partner is known to have at least 14.

―――――

As South you hold:

♠ x x x
♡ A J x x x (5) + 1 rebid point
♢ K Q x   (5)
♣ x x   (1)

The bidding has proceeded:

North	South
1 Spade	2 Hearts
3 Hearts	?

You should bid 4 Hearts. Your hand has a rebid value of 12 points. Partner by opening and raising to 3 has shown a good hand (about 16 points).

―――――

As South you hold:

♠ K Q 10 x (5)
♡ K Q x x (5)
♢ A x   (5)
♣ x x x

The bidding has proceeded:

North	South
1 Diamond	1 Spade
3 Spades	?

This hand has the value of 15 points. North has shown a holding ranging from 16 to 19, placing you in the slam zone. You should bid 4 Diamonds, showing the Ace and await your partner's reaction. This is a very probable slam.

———

As South you hold:

♠ x x   (1)
♡ A K J x x   (8) + 1 rebid point
◇ K Q x   (5)
♣ J 10 x   (1)

The bidding has proceeded:

North	South
1 Spade	2 Hearts
4 Hearts	?

Slam is in the air. Your hand has a rebid value of 16 points. Partner has opened and jumped in your suit, which marks him with a strong hand, probably 17 points or more. This adds up to enough count for a slam. You may check for Aces. A 4 No Trump bid at this point is a clear cut Blackwood bid and would protect you against partner's holding some hand like this:

♠ A K Q x x
♡ Q 10 x x
◊ x
♣ K Q x

As South you hold:

♠ A K J x x
♡ J x
◊ x x x
♣ K Q x

The bidding has proceeded:

North	South
1 Heart	1 Spade
2 No Trump	?

You have enough to warrant contraction for slam. Partner has promised at least 19 points. You have a high card count of 14, accounting for the required 33. In addition you have the following bullish features: a good five card suit to work with—the Jack of Hearts may be quite valuable. Bid 6 No Trump.

As South you hold:

♠ K x x
♡ x x
◊ A K 10 x x
♣ x x x

The bidding has proceeded:

North	South
1 Spade	2 Diamonds
2 No Trump	?

What do you bid now?

Answer: 3 Spades. Since partner has announced a holding of at least 16 points you know that you have enough for game, but you should give partner the choice between 4 Spades and 3 No Trump. Your 3 Spade bid is forcing, for partner can recognize that your team has 26 points. He knows he has 16 and since you responded with two of a new suit, he knows you have at least 10.

CHAPTER XIV

Overcalls

IN MAKING overcalls (i.e., when an opponent has opened the bidding) too much reliance should not be placed on point count. The consideration of paramount importance is the texture of your trump suit. When you overcall at the level of 2, you should promise partner that you won't lose more than two tricks in the trump suit itself.

Opponent opens 1 Spade. You hold:

(A)			(B)	
♠ x x x		♠ x x		(1)
♡ A x	(5)	♡ K Q J 9 x x	(6)
◇ K x x	(3)	◇ A x x	(4)
♣ A Q x x x	(6)	♣ x x	(1)

Hand (A) is valued at 14 points (13 in high cards and 1 for doubleton). Hand (B) has the value of only 12 points (10 in high cards and 1 each for the doubletons). Yet hand (B) is a much better overcall, for you are in a position to promise that you will not lose more than two trump tricks if you overcall with 2 Hearts.

With hand (A), (call me a timid soul if you choose), I would not overcall with 2 Clubs. I could very easily lose three or four tricks in Clubs alone.

When I overcall, I like to make sure that if doubled I won't go down more than 500 points. There is nothing like 800 or 1100 sets to impair one's social standing. To overcall at the level of 2 one must be working with a good trump suit, or on a liberal cash allowance.

The prime inducement for making an overcall is to suggest a good lead to partner. That's why overcalls on Jack-high suits stand in such little favor.

Opponent opens 1 Diamond. You hold:

	(A)			(B)	
♠	x x x		♠	x x x	
♡	J 9 x x x	(1)	♡	K Q J x x	(6)
♢	A x	(5)	♢	x x	(1)
♣	K J x	(4)	♣	K x x	(3)

Both hands are valued at 10 points. I would overcall 1 Heart with (B) but not with (A).

An overcall of 1 No Trump should be based on a hand that would have been a sound opening 1 No Trump bid (16 to 19 points), and the adverse suit must be safely stopped.

To summarize: To overcall at the level of one you should have at least 10 points. But the mere possession of 10 points does not justify an overcall.

To overcall at the level of two you should have at least 12 points and a very good suit.

CHAPTER XV

The Take-out Double

THOUGH THE subject is not at all complex, considerable difficulty seems to be experienced by many Bridge players in the handling of this weapon. A condition which, it seems to me, can be rectified by just a bit of study.

When an opponent opens the bidding, more than average strength can be announced in several ways. The most usual is the take-out double.

"Partner, don't be intimidated by the opening bidder. My hand is probably as good as his. At any rate, it will make a good dummy." That is the message the take-out double is intended to convey. In other words, a take-out double shows a hand that is at least as good as an opening bid. That is to say, it should contain at least 13 points.

Your right hand opponent opens with 1 Club. You hold:

	(A)			(B)	
♠	A 10 x x	(4)	♠	A K J x x	(8)
♡	K 9 x x	(3)	♡	A 10 x x	(4)
◇	K J x x	(4)	◇	x x x	
♣	x	(2)	♣	x	(2)
		13			14

Holding either of these hands you should double. Many players will be shocked at the suggestion that hand (A), under the circumstances, is a proper take-out double. Those players have gotten into the habit of insisting upon three honor tricks for a take-out double. Conversely, and what is a more objectionable practice, they double willy-nilly when they hold three honor tricks. Observe the following two cases:

(C)		(D)	
♠ x x x		♠ x x x	
♡ A K x	(7)	♡ A K x	(7)
♢ A x x	(4)	♢ A Q x	(6)
♣ x x x x		♣ x x x x	

Your right hand opponent has opened the bidding with 1 Spade, what should you do?

In both cases you should pass.

Hand (C) contains but 11 points—hand (D) contains 13 points. But since these hands will have to be dummy for partner, it is sound policy to deduct a point from each for its flaw. They have the defect of possessing a 4-3-3-3 distribution as a prospective dummy. Proper application of the point count in this situation will actually safeguard the less experienced player against certain errors in judgment.

Possession of 13 or more points by the player contemplating a take-out double will usually, but not necessarily, protect against these errors in judgment. However, it must be borne in mind that the doubler, in addition to having the required point count, must promise partner that his hand will be a good dummy. Either that, or the doubler must have a reasonably safe contract in mind. In a word, the take-out doubler must promise safety. Observe the following case:

♠ A Q x x   (6)
♡ x   (2)
♢ A x x x   (4)
♣ A J x x   (5)
                ——
                17

Your right hand opponent opened the bidding with 1 Spade. Despite the fact that your hand has a value of 17 points, it would not be a sound take-out double inasmuch as you must be prepared for partner's expected response of 2 Hearts. In that case your hand would not be a good dummy, and you have not the high card values to justify a bid of 2 No Trump, which would be your only out. There is nothing left for you to do, therefore, but to make a trap pass.

Had your right hand opponent opened with 1 Heart your hand would have been an ideal double. It would also have been suitable for a take-out double if the adverse bid had been 1 Club or 1 Diamond; for, if partner made the expected response of 1 Heart, you would at least be in a position where you might escape with reasonable safety to 1 Spade.

Be careful of take-out doubles with evenly balanced hands. Remember you must subtract a point in that case if you hold a 4-3-3-3.

Be careful, too, about doubling when your principal strength is in the adverse suit.

Take-Out Double of 1 No Trump

A take-out double should represent a hand that is presumably as strong as the opening bidder's. Therefore, when making an immediate double of 1 No Trump you should

have at least 16 points in high cards. LEAVE IN AN IM-
MEDIATE DOUBLE OF 1 NO TRUMP IF YOU
HAVE AT LEAST 6 POINTS IN HIGH CARDS. For
example:

As South you hold:

> ♠ 10 x
> ♡ x x x
> ◇ Q x x   (2)
> ♣ K J x x x (4)

The bidding has proceeded:

West	North	East	South
1 No Trump	Double	Pass	?

You should pass. Here is the arithmetic: partner has at
least 16, you have 6; the partnership, therefore, has at least
22 points, whereas the opponents have at most 18. Bear in
mind that the opening bidder's dummy will have at most 2
points and perhaps less. Since you outnumber them in
count, you will win more tricks than they and you should
play for the penalty.

Take-Out Double to Reopen the Bidding

This bid may be made with as little as 11 points. For
example:

As South you hold:

> ♠ A x x x   (4)
> ♡ K x x x   (3)
> ◇ K J x   (4)
> ♣ x x   (1)
> $\overline{}$
> 12

The bidding has proceeded:

West	North	East	South
1 Club	Pass	Pass	?

With this hand you may double to reopen the bidding in order to permit your side to try for the part score. Doubler's partner should view the take-out double in this situation with some measure of suspicion, unless doubler confirms the soundness of his double by subsequent action.

CHAPTER XVI

Responses to the Take-out Double

A NATURAL tendency of players is to undervalue their hands as responder to a take-out double. This table is recommended to assist you in forming an estimate of your holding.

A hand containing 6 points is a fair hand.

A hand containing 9 points is a good hand.

A hand containing 11 points is a probable game hand.

Partner doubles 1 Heart. You hold:

(A)			(B)		
♠ A J x x x	(5)		♠ A J x x x	(5)	
♡ x x x			♡ x x x		
◇ x x x			◇ K x x	(3)	
♣ x x	(1)		♣ x x	(1)	
	6			9	

(C)			(D)		
♠ A J x x x	(5)		♠ A J x x x x	(5)	
♡ x x x			♡ x x x		
◇ K Q x	(5)		◇ K J x	(4)	
♣ x x	(1)		♣ x	(2)	
	11			11	

(A) contains 6 points and is a fair hand.

(B) contains 9 points and is a good hand.

(C) and (D) contain 11 points each and, therefore, are probable game hands. You should respond with one more than is necessary, that is, 2 Spades.

The requirement for responding to partner's take-out double is *zero points*. The less you have, the more urgent it is to respond, else opponents will make their doubled contract with overtricks, which can prove very costly.

In responding to partner's take-out double prefer a four card major to a five card minor at the level of 1. For example:

♠ K x x x
♡ x x
♢ Q 10 x x x
♣ x x

Partner doubles 1 Heart. Respond 1 Spade rather than 2 Diamonds.

Your partner doubles 1 Diamond. You hold:

♠ K J x x   (4)
♡ A J x x   (5)
♢ x x x
♣ x x   (1)
          ——
          10

Your hand has the value of 10 points. It is, therefore, a *good* hand. You should arrange to bid both suits in their logical order, showing Spades first.

In responding to a take-out double prefer a major suit to 1 No Trump, but prefer 1 No Trump to a minor suit if you hold a fairly good hand, that is, about 9 points in high cards. With only a single stopper in the suit bid by opponents it is perhaps more prudent to insist upon 10 points for a 1 No Trump response. For example, partner doubles a bid of 1 Heart, and you hold:

$$
\begin{array}{lll}
\spadesuit & x\ x & \\
\heartsuit & Q\ J\ 9\ x & (3) \\
\diamondsuit & A\ 9\ x & (4) \\
\clubsuit & Q\ 10\ x\ x & \underline{(2)} \\
& & 9
\end{array}
$$

Your best response is 1 No Trump. This hand contains 9 points, with a double Heart stopper. This is preferable to responding with 2 Clubs.

Your partner doubles 1 Heart. You hold:

$$
\begin{array}{lll}
\spadesuit & Q\ 9\ x\ x & (2) \\
\heartsuit & K\ Q\ x & (5) \\
\diamondsuit & Q\ x\ x & (2) \\
\clubsuit & x\ x\ x & \underline{} \\
& & 9
\end{array}
$$

While the hand has the strength to justify a 1 No Trump response to partner's double, that is, 9 points, a bid of 1 Spade is to be preferred.

If you have a fair hand you should bid again when partner jumps.

With a good hand you should bid again if partner takes any moderate action.

With 13 points, drastic action is mandatory. Make a bid which is absolutely forcing to game.

Even with 12 points, game will probably be reached and strong action is indicated.

Partner doubles 1 Club. You hold:

♠ K x x x   (3)
♡ A x x   (4)
♦ K Q x   (5)
♣ x x x
             ___
             12

You have 12 points which should convince you that there is a game for your side and a jump response is indicated. Bid 2 Spades despite the weakness of the suit.

Your partner doubles 1 Club. You hold.

♠ K J x   (4)
♡ x x x
♦ Q J x x   (3)
♣ K Q x   (5)
             ___
             12

Holding 12 points you should make a jump response of 2 No Trump.

Notice this is a point less than is required for a 2 No Trump response to an opening suit bid. The reason is that your 2 No Trump bid in this sequence is not 100% forcing. If the take-out double has been shaded the doubler may take the liberty of passing.

Business Pass of Partner's Take-Out Double

Don't pass partner's take-out double of 1 of a suit unless you are quite sure you will show a profit by doing so. Don't get panicky because you have a bad hand. When you speak in this position you are not making a bid in the true sense of the word. You are merely replying to partner's question, "What is your best suit, however weak it may be?" In order to justify passing his double you must have a reasonable expectancy of winning four tricks; and at least three of them should be in the trump suit.

This is not to be confused with a business pass of partner's immediate double of 1 No Trump. Such a double may be left in if you have 6 points.

Procedure by Doubler's Partner After an Intervening Bid

A free response should be made if doubler's partner holds a fairly good hand, that is, about 8 points, counting both high cards and distribution. Remember, a hand containing 6 points is a fair hand and a hand containing 9 points is a good hand. 8 points, therefore, would make a fairly good hand.

As South you hold:

(A)		(B)	
♠ A J x x x	(5)	♠ Q J x x x	(3)
♡ x x x		♡ x x x	
◇ Q x x	(2)	◇ K J x	(4)
♣ x x	(1)	♣ x x	(1)
	8		8

The bidding has proceeded:

West	North	East	South
1 Club	Double	1 Heart	?

With either of these hands you should make a free bid of
1 Spade. You have 8 points—7 in high cards and 1 for distribution—so you have a hand which justifies a free bid at
the level of 1. If your free bid must be at a higher level you
will require slightly more strength.

As South you hold:

$$
\begin{array}{ll}
\spadesuit \ A \ Q \ x \ x & (6) \\
\heartsuit \ x \ x & (1) \\
\diamondsuit \ K \ x \ x \ x & (3) \\
\clubsuit \ x \ x \ x & \\
\hline
& 10
\end{array}
$$

The bidding has proceeded:

West	North	East	South
1 Heart	Double	2 Hearts	?

Your hand has the value of 10 points, and you should make
a free bid of 2 Spades.

Raises by Doubler

The doubler should exercise caution in offering raises to
a partner whom he has forced to bid.

As South you hold:

$$
\begin{array}{l}
\spadesuit \ A \ Q \ x \ x \\
\heartsuit \ K \ Q \ x \ x \\
\diamondsuit \ x \\
\clubsuit \ Q \ x \ x \ x
\end{array}
$$

The bidding has proceeded:

East	South	West	North
1 Diamond	Double	Pass	1 Spade
Pass	?		

You should raise only to 2 Spades. Remember, partner may have no values.

The above hand was valued at 15 points when you doubled—13 in high cards and 2 for distribution. However, since partner has responded in a suit which you can well support, you may revalue your hand as dummy; the singleton, therefore, becomes worth 3 points in the dummy hand (whereas it would have been valued at only 2 points in the hand of the initial bidder).

The following is a reasonably accurate guide for a doubler who is contemplating a raise of his partner's forced take-out:

> With 16 points he may go to the 2 level
>
> With 19 points he may go to the 3 level
>
> With 22 points he may go to the 4 level

Action by Opener's Partner Over a Double

Before proceeding any further into this subject let me caution you against a popular superstition to the effect that "a bid over a double shows weakness." It doesn't do so any more than it shows your political affiliation.

What you should do when partner's opening bid has been doubled depends on the type of hand you hold. Briefly, here is the practice:

With a good hand you redouble. This may be done even

without support for partner's suit. What constitutes a good hand? One that is above average in high cards, or which, because of distribution, is worth more than one bid. Remember, so far as responder is concerned, the indifferent hands range from 6 to 10 points—when they are above that strength, responder has a good hand and must plan to bid more. He must, therefore, make a one round force. The redouble serves that purpose, and assures him another opportunity to bid. Unless the opposition is indiscreet enough to let the hand play at one redoubled, which should be a tasty enough morsel.

With a weak hand you *pass,* except that you are permitted to give partner a raise if adequate trump support is held, just to get into the other fellow's hair.

With hands of mediocre value, (anything up to about 9 or 10 points), it is better strategy to bid early and avoid the rush.

Partner opens 1 Heart. Next hand doubles. You hold:

(1) ♠ A J x x   (2) ♠ x x
     ♡ x   ♡ J x x
     ◊ K J x x   ◊ A x x x x
     ♣ K J x x   ♣ K Q x

(3) ♠ x x   (4) ♠ x
     ♡ Q x x x   ♡ Q x x x x
     ◊ K x x x   ◊ K x x x x
     ♣ x x x   ♣ x x

         (5) ♠ A J x x x
              ♡ x x
              ◊ K x x
              ♣ x x x

(1) Redouble, though you have no support for partner's suit. Your hand is above average in high cards. In fact it has a value in high cards alone of 13 points.

(2) Redouble, in support of Hearts. This hand has a value of 11 points.

(3) Raise to 2 Hearts. This may be done on relatively weak holdings. This hand has a valuation of 7.

(4) Bid 3 Hearts—a barricade raise made in an attempt to embarrass the opposition. Such a bid usually shows about 8 to 10 points in support.

(5) Bid 1 Spade. This hand is not strong enough to re-double. It is worth only 9 points.

Conversely—as South you hold:

♠ A K 10 x
♡ x x x
♢ A K x
♣ x x x

The bidding has proceeded:

South	West	North	East
1 Spade	Double	3 Spades	Pass

What do you bid?

You should pass. Your hand has the value of 14 points. In order to produce game partner would have to contribute 12 points, which he has denied holding. If he had 11 points he would have redoubled. North is simply trying to make a pest of himself to the opponents and so far has succeeded.

IN BRIEF

A take-out double should be based on a hand of the same strength as an opening bid, that is, 13 points.

An immediate double of 1 No Trump should therefore be based on 16 points.

When partner responds in a suit for which you have good support, revalue your hand as dummy.

As responder to a take-out double: if you have 6 points you have a fair hand, 9 points a good hand, and 11 points a probable game.

As partner of the opening bidder, after a take-out double, pass with a poor hand, redouble with a good hand, and bid immediately with a moderate hand.

CHAPTER XVII

Penalty Doubles

THE POINT COUNT is not a complete guide for purposes of making penalty doubles in suit bids. But in making penalty doubles of No Trump contracts it may be applied with deadly accuracy.

In making these computations, when partner has opened with 1 of a suit, it is presumed that he has at least 13 points. By adding your values to those announced by partner, a rough estimate may be made of the comparative strength of the two teams.

Likewise at No Trump where your side outweighs the enemy by 4 or 5 points, you should be able to beat them at a 1 No Trump contract, since your side should win more tricks, e.g.,

Your partner opens 1 Spade. Right hand opponent overcalls with 1 No Trump. You hold:

♠ Q x x
♡ 10 x x x
◊ A J x
♣ K x x

Without even considering the promoted value of the Queen of Spades you have 10 points—13 + 10 = 23. You outweigh the enemy by at least 23 to 17 and a penalty double is in order.

It may be argued that a considerable portion of the opening bidder's 13 points may consist of distributional values—

that is, singletons and doubletons, which are not helpful in defense of No Trump contracts. The answer is that in such cases the opening bidder should realize that his hand is unsuitable defensively, and he should not stand for the double of a low contract, e.g.,

As South you hold:

♠ A Q x x x x x
♡ x x
◇ K J x
♣ x

The bidding has proceeded:

South	West	North	East
1 Spade	1 No Trump	Double	Pass
?			

You should rebid 2 Spades, since your hand is unsuitable defensively.

With a good five card suit you may double a 1 No Trump bid with a point less, e.g.,

Your partner opens 1 Spade. Right hand opponent overcalls with 1 No Trump. You hold:

♠ x x x
♡ x x
◇ x x x
♣ A K Q x x

You should double; $13 + 9 = 22$ (plus a five card suit). Opponents have at most 18.

A fairly accurate guide is this: When your partner opens the bidding and your right hand opponent overcalls with that suit which it was your desire to bid, double for keeps. The technique is to count the number of tricks you expect partner to produce. (Experience has shown that the normal opening bid of 1 in a suit will produce about three tricks in the defensive play.) Then on the fingers of your left hand count the number you expect to contribute, add them together, and "let her go."

As South you hold:

> ♠ x x
> ♡ A x x x
> ◇ K J 9 x
> ♣ x x x

The bidding has proceeded:

North	East	South
1 Spade	2 Diamonds	?

Double. You may expect to win three tricks in Diamonds and one in Hearts. The opener may be relied upon to develop three tricks. This comes to seven. A two trick penalty is anticipated. You must not fall into the error of calling 2 No Trump, with a hand that contains only 8 points in high cards.

QUIZZES

(Answers on pages 131 to 146)

QUIZ NO. 1

As dealer you hold the following hands. What is your opening bid?

(1) ♠ x x x
♡ A K x x
◊ x x x
♣ A K x

(2) ♠ A 10 x x
♡ A x x x
◊ x x
♣ A x x

(3) ♠ A K x
♡ 10 x x
◊ x x x
♣ A J x x

(4) ♠ K x x x x
♡ A x x
◊ A x x
♣ x x

(5) ♠ A Q x x x
♡ A x x
◊ J x x
♣ x x

(6) ♠ A Q 10 x x x
♡ x
◊ K J x x
♣ x x

115

(7) ♠ A 10 9 x x   (9) ♠ K Q x
     ♡ K 10 x x x   ♡ A x x
     ◇ none   ◇ A x x
     ♣ K J x   ♣ Q x x x

(8) ♠ A J x x   (10) ♠ A K x
     ♡ A K x   ♡ A Q x
     ◇ x x x   ◇ K Q x
     ♣ x x x   ♣ Q x x x

Grade yourself: (9 or 10) Excellent, (8) Very good, (7) Good. If you score under 7 we advise rereading Chapter I.

QUIZ NO. 2

As dealer you hold the following hands. What would you bid?

(1) ♠ K J 10
    ♡ K Q 10
    ◊ A J x
    ♣ A J 10 x

(4) ♠ A K Q x
    ♡ Q J 9 x x
    ◊ K x
    ♣ A x

(2) ♠ A 10 x x x x x
    ♡ none
    ◊ x
    ♣ A J x x x

(5) ♠ A K 10 9
    ♡ A
    ◊ K Q 10 x
    ♣ K Q J x

(3) ♠ A K J x
    ♡ Q J x x x
    ◊ x
    ♣ Q x x

(6) ♠ A K Q
    ♡ A Q J 9
    ◊ K Q 10
    ♣ A K Q

(7) ♠ K Q J
♡ A K J x x
◊ A x
♣ A K x

(9) ♠ A K J 10 x
♡ x
◊ x x
♣ K x x x x

(8) ♠ K Q J x x x x
♡ A x
◊ A K x x
♣ none

(10) ♠ A K J 10 x x x
♡ x x
◊ x x
♣ A Q

Grade yourself: (9 or 10) Excellent, (8) Very good, (7) Good. Under 7, reread Chapters I, II, IV.

QUIZ NO. 3

What is your response? Partner opens with 1 Heart. You hold:

(1) ♠ 10 x
  ♡ A J x x
  ◊ K J x x
  ♣ Q x x

(4) ♠ K Q
  ♡ K Q 10 x
  ◊ J 10 x x
  ♣ A K 10

(2) ♠ x
  ♡ K 10 x x
  ◊ A x x x
  ♣ A K Q x

(5) ♠ K x x
  ♡ Q J x x x
  ◊ A J x
  ♣ x x

(3) ♠ A 10 x
  ♡ K J 10 x x
  ◊ x x x
  ♣ x x

(6) ♠ K Q 10 x
  ♡ K J 10
  ◊ x x x
  ♣ J x x

E

(7) ♠ J x x x
    ♡ x x
    ◊ Q 10 x x
    ♣ Q x x

(9) ♠ K J x
    ♡ x x x x
    ◊ x x
    ♣ A Q x x

(8) ♠ x x x
    ♡ J 9 x
    ◊ A x
    ♣ K 10 x x x

(10) ♠ K J x
    ♡ x x x x
    ◊ x x
    ♣ A J x x

Grade yourself: (9 or 10) Excellent, (8) Very good, (7) Good. Under 7, reread Chapter IX.

QUIZ NO. 4

Partner opens 1 Heart. You hold:

(1) ♠ J x x
     ♡ Q x   1 NT
     ◇ x x x
     ♣ A Q 9 x x

(2) ♠ A x x
     ♡ x x   1 NT
     ◇ K x x x
     ♣ A x x x

(3) ♠ K 10 x x
     ♡ A x x   3 NT
     ◇ K x x
     ♣ A Q x

What is your response?

Partner opens 1 No Trump. You hold:

(4) ♠ Q x x x
     ♡ K x x   2 NT
     ◇ K x x x
     ♣ 10 x

(5) ♠ 10 x x
     ♡ Q x x x x   P
     ◇ x x x
     ♣ Q x

(6) ♠ A Q 10 x x   3
     ♡ 10 x x x
     ◇ K J x
     ♣ x

What is your response?

Partner opens 2 No Trump. You hold:

(7) ♠ x x x x   (8) ♠ K x x
   ♥ Q 10 x x x x   ♥ J 10 x
   ♦ x x   ♦ A Q J
   ♣ x   ♣ Q J 10 x

(9) ♠ A Q x
   ♥ K 10 x
   ♦ K Q J x x
   ♣ x x

What is your response?

Grade yourself: (9) Excellent, (8) Very good, (7) Good. Under 7, reread Chapters V, IX.

QUIZ NO. 5

You are South. What do you bid?

(1) ♠ x x
    ♡ K Q x
    ◇ A K J x
    ♣ A Q x x

S.	W.	N.	E.
1 D.	P.	1 S.	P.
?			

(2) ♠ J x
    ♡ K Q 10
    ◇ A K J x
    ♣ A Q J x

S.	W.	N.	E.
1 D.	P.	1 S.	P.
?			

(3) ♠ x x x
    ♡ A x x
    ◇ A K x x
    ♣ A 10 x

S.	W.	N.	E.
1 D.	P.	1 S.	P.
?			

(4) ♠ J x
    ♡ A K J x x
    ◇ K x x
    ♣ Q x x

S.	W.	N.	E.
1 H.	P.	1 NT	P.
?			

(5) ♠ K Q 10 x x
    ♡ x x
    ◇ x x x
    ♣ A K x

S.	W.	N.	E.
1 S.	P.	2 NT	P.
?			

(6) ♠ A K 10 x x
    ♡ A J 9 x
    ◇ K 10 x
    ♣ x

S.	W.	N.	E.
1 S.	P.	1 NT	P.
?			

(7) ♠ 10 x   (8) ♠ 10 x
    ♡ A x x x   ♡ A x x x
    ◇ A J 10 x x   ◇ A Q 10 x x
    ♣ A x   ♣ A K

S.	W.	N.	E.		S.	W.	N.	E.
1 D.	P.	1 H.	P.		1 D.	P.	1 H.	P.
?					?			

(9) ♠ A K x x x x
    ♡ x x x
    ◇ x
    ♣ A J x

S.	W.	N.	E.
1 S.	P.	2 S.	P.
?			

Grade yourself: (9) Excellent, (8) Very good, (7) Good. Under 7, reread Chapter XII.

QUIZ NO. 6

What do you bid? You are South and hold:

(1) ♠ Q x x
   ♡ A Q x x
   ◇ K x x
   ♣ Q 10 x

N.	E.	S.	W.
1 C.	P.	1 H.	P.
1 NT	P.	?	

(2) ♠ Q J 9 x
   ♡ x x
   ◇ K 9 x x x
   ♣ J x

N.	E.	S.	W.
1 C.	P.	1 D.	P.
1 H.	P.	?	

(3) ♠ K J 9 x
   ♡ x x
   ◇ x x x
   ♣ A Q x x

N.	E.	S.	W.
1 D.	P.	1 S.	P.
2 S.	P.	?	

(4) ♠ A K x
   ♡ J x x
   ◇ A x x x
   ♣ A x x

S.	W.	N.	E.
1 NT	P.	4 H.	P.
?			

(5) ♠ J x x x
   ♡ K Q x x
   ◇ x x
   ♣ A x x

S.	W.	N.	E.
P.	P.	1 D.	P.
1 H.	P.	1 S.	P.
?			

(6) ♠ A J x x x
   ♡ x x
   ◇ K x x
   ♣ x x x

N.	E.	S.
1 H.	Do.	?

(7) ♠ K Q 10
   ♡ A K J 9
   ◇ A K Q J 10
   ♣ x

S.	W.	N.	E.
2 D.	P.	2 H.	P.
?			

(8) ♠ A K Q J x x
   ♡ A x
   ◇ A K Q 10
   ♣ x

S.	W.	N.	E.
2 S.	P.	2 NT	P.
3 D.	P.	3 S.	P.
?			

(9) ♠ x x
   ♡ Q x
   ◇ Q J 10 x
   ♣ A Q 9 x x

N.	E.	S.	W.
1 H.	P.	2 C.	P.
3 C.	P.	?	

Grade yourself: (9) Excellent, (8) Very good, (7) Good. Under 7, reread Chapters VI, XII, XIII, XV, XVI.

QUIZ NO. 7

What do you bid? As South you hold:

(1) ♠ A K x x x
   ♡ K x x
   ◊ K 10 x
   ♣ A Q

S.	W.	N.	E.
1 S.	P.	3 S.	P.
?			

(2) ♠ x x
   ♡ K J x x
   ◊ A 10 x
   ♣ J 9 x x

N.	E.	S.
1 NT	2 S.	?

(3) ♠ J x
   ♡ K 10 x
   ◊ A K J x
   ♣ K x x x

S.	W.	N.	E.
1 D.	1 S.	1 NT	P.
?			

(4) ♠ K J 10 x
   ♡ x x x
   ◊ x x x
   ♣ A Q x

N.	E.	S.
1 S.	P.	?

(5) ♠ 10 x x
   ♡ x
   ◊ A x x x x
   ♣ K x x x

N.	E.	S.
1 S.	P.	?

(6) ♠ A x x
   ♡ J 10 x x x
   ◊ x x x
   ♣ A K

N.	E.	S.
1 H.	P.	?

(7) ♠ A K J x x   (8) ♠ A 9 x x x x
    ♡ x x x   ♡ K J x
    ◇ x x   ◇ Q x x
    ♣ A x x   ♣ A

S.   W.   N.   E.   S.   W.   N.   E.
1 S. P.   2 D. P.   1 S. P.   2 H. P.
2 S. P.   3 S. P.   ?
 ?

(9) ♠ K Q x x
    ♡ x
    ◇ A 10 x x
    ♣ K 10 x x

    N.   E.   S.
    1 H. Do.   ?

Grade yourself: (9) Excellent, (8) Very good, (7) Good. Under 7, reread Chapters V, IX, XII.

QUIZ NO. 8

What do you bid? You are South and hold:

(1) ♠ K x
♥ A Q x
♦ A Q 9 x x
♣ K x x

N.	E.	S.
P.	P.	?

(4) ♠ none
♥ x x x x
♦ A Q J x x x
♣ Q x x

N.	E.	S.	W.
2 C.	P.	2 D.	P.
2 S.	P.	3 D.	P.
3 S.	P.	?	

(2) ♠ K 10 x x x
♥ x
♦ A x x x
♣ J x x

N.	E.	S.
1 NT	P.	?

(5) ♠ A K Q J x
♥ A K x
♦ A J 9 x
♣ x

S.	W.	N.	E.
2 S.	P.	2 NT	3 C.
?			

(3) ♠ A K x
♥ A K x
♦ x x x
♣ A K x x

S.	W.	N.	E.
1 C.	P.	1 H.	P.
?			

(6) ♠ J 10 x x
♥ x
♦ K x x x
♣ Q J x x

S.	W.	N.	E.
P.	P.	1 H.	Do.
?			

(7) ♠ J x x   (8) ♠ J x x
    ♡ A K x x   ♡ x x
    ◇ x   ◇ A x x
    ♣ K Q x x x   ♣ A K x x x

S.	W.	N.	E.		N.	E.	S.
1 C.	P.	1 D.	P.		P.	1 S.	?
1 H.	P.	1 NT	P.				
?							

(9) ♠ Q J x x
    ♡ Q x x x
    ◇ J x x x
    ♣ x

N.	E.	S.
2 S.	P.	?

Grade yourself: (9) Excellent, (8) Very good, (7) Good. Under 7, reread Chapters II, IV, V, IX, XI, XII.

1. 1 Club. This hand, containing 14 points, is a mandatory opening. The Club bid is chosen for convenience. If you open with 1 Heart, no convenient rebid will be available if partner responds 2 Diamonds.

2. This hand contains 13 points, 12 in high cards and 1 for the doubleton. It is, therefore, an optional opening. Inasmuch as the hand contains eight cards in the major suits and a rebid can be arranged for, the option to open should be exercised. You have a choice between 1 Spade, reserving 2 Hearts as a rebid, or you may open with 1 Club. If partner responds with 1 of a major suit, you will raise. If he responds with 1 Diamond, you may rebid at the level of 1 in a major suit.

3. This hand contains only 12 points, and normally should be passed. However, if you choose to open with 1 Club no criticism can be found, for a convenient rebid is available to you at 1 No Trump, if partner responds with 1 of a suit.

4. Pass. This hand contains only 12 points, 11 in high cards and 1 for the doubleton. Since no convenient rebid is available, an opening would be bad strategy.

5. Pass. This hand contains 12 points, but the Spade suit is not good enough to offer a comfortable rebid. If the Jack of Diamonds were moved out into the Spade suit, you would have an optional opening, for the Spade suit would then be rebiddable.

6. 1 Spade. This hand has a value of 13 points; 10 in high cards, 2 for the singleton and 1 for the doubleton. A convenient rebid is available in this very good Spade suit.

7.   1 Spade. This hand has a value of 14 points, and is, therefore, a mandatory opening. It has 11 points in high cards, and 3 points for the void. The rebid over 2 Diamonds will be 2 Hearts.

8.   Pass. This hand contains only 12 points, and has no convenient rebid.

9.   1 Club. This has the right shape for 1 No Trump, but counts only 15 points, and is therefore an eyelash short.

10.   1 Club. This hand is the proper design for a 1 No Trump bid, but it is slightly too strong, counting 20 points in high cards. If partner responds with 1 of a suit, you may jump to 2 No Trump next round.

QUIZ No. 2

1.   1 Club. This hand is just a shade too strong for 1 No Trump. It contains 19 points, plus three 10's. While we have not chosen to assign specific values to 10's, they cannot be ignored completely. 19 is the top limit for a 1 No Trump opening, and if any 10's are held in addition, the hand should be considered as too strong for the 1 No Trump bid. Inasmuch as we haven't brought this up before, take half credit if your answer was 1 No Trump.

2.   1 Spade. This is a mandatory opening, having a value of 14 points; 9 in high cards, 3 for the void, and 2 for the singleton.

3.   1 Spade. This hand has a value of 15 points, and is therefore, one of moderate strength. You should, therefore, plan to show both suits at a reasonable level. This may be done only by pretending that the Hearts and Spades are the same length.

4. 1 Heart. This is a very powerful hand, having a value of 21 points, and an accurate description should be given of its distribution since there is no fear of reaching the high level with a hand of this strength.

5. 1 Diamond. This has the proper high card strength, 22 points, for an opening 2 No Trump bid, but it does not have the right shape. Despite the six honor tricks, give no thought to opening with a demand bid of 2. Remember that the hand has an adjusted value of only 24 points with Diamonds as trumps.

6. This hand has a value of 30 points, and is, therefore, too big for an opening bid of 3 No Trump. Our choice is for a bid of 2 Hearts. If partner makes the expected response of 2 No Trump, our next bid will be 4 No Trump. This is not a Blackwood call, but denotes a hand with which the opener will surely win ten tricks. If responder has the sign of a trick taking possibility, such as a King, he should raise.

7. 2 Hearts. This hand has a value of 26 points; 25 in high cards, and 1 for the doubleton.

8. 2 Spades. This hand has only four losers, and the necessary high card strength. It will be observed that the hand has a value of 21 points; 17 in high cards, 3 for the void, and 1 for the doubleton. An opening 2 bid may be made with 21 points, if you have a good seven card suit.

9. 1 Spade. Intending to rebid 2 Spades over 2 of a red suit or 1 No Trump, ignoring the emaciated Club suit in favor of the strong major suit with honors.

10. 1 Spade. Do not make the mistake of pre-empting because of the long Spade suit. This hand has a perfectly sound opening 1 bid, and a pre-empt would be improper.

QUIZ No. 3

1. 2 Diamonds. This hand has a value of 12 points, 11 in high cards and 1 for the doubleton Spade, and is, therefore, too good for a single raise. However, it has not strength enough for a jump to 3 Hearts, which would require 13 points. You must arrange to bid twice. A temporizing bid of 2 Diamonds is chosen, with the intention of supporting Hearts next round.

2. 3 Clubs. This hand has a value of 20 points, 17 in high cards, and 3 for the singleton Spade. Add that to partner's expected 13, and you have 33, suggesting a very probable slam. It is poor tactics to respond 3 Hearts on this hand. A 3 Heart bid denotes a hand ranging in value from 13 to 16.

3. 2 Hearts. Don't be excited by the fifth Heart. This hand has a value of only 9 points, 8 in high cards and 1 for the doubleton Club.

4. 3 Clubs. This hand has a value of 19 points, 18 in high cards and 1 for the doubleton Spade. Such holdings suggest slam possibilities if partner has slightly more than a minimum, and the jump shift should be made in a "manufactured" suit.

5. 3 Hearts. This is just the right size. The hand has a value of 13 points. 12 in high cards (Q J = 4 in Trump), and 1 for the doubleton Club.

6. 2 Hearts. This is preferable to responding with 1 Spade, since the hand is worth only one forward bid. On the surface it counts 10 points. However, its true value is only 9, since a point must be deducted for the infirmity of the 4-3-3-3 distribution.

7. Pass. This hand has only 5 points in high cards. Therefore, it does not qualify for a response of 1 No Trump. We sometimes shade the requirement in making a one over one response, but we prefer not to do so in a non-biddable suit, with a sub-minimum holding.

8. 2 Hearts. The hand is not quite strong enough for a 2 Club bid, and 1 No Trump is not preferred with this particular type holding. The single raise is, therefore, in order. This hand is, on the surface, worth 10 points, but a point must be deducted because you hold only three trumps, so that it comes well within the range of a single raise.

9. 2 Clubs. This hand has a value of 11 points, 10 in high cards and 1 for the doubleton Diamond. It is, therefore, worth two bids, and is too strong for a single raise. Hearts will be supported next round.

10. This hand has a value of 10 points, and is therefore, on the borderline between a maximum single raise and a hand worth two bids. This is what is known as one of the judgment points, and which step to take is entirely up to you. With an aggressive partner, you may choose to bid merely 2 Hearts, knowing that he will probably act again if his hand contains 16 points. With a partner who normally requires prodding, perhaps it would be better tactics to respond 2 Clubs, reserving a Heart raise for the next round.

QUIZ No. 4

1. **2 Clubs.** Had the opening bid been a Diamond, our choice would have been for a response of 1 No Trump, for the hand has a high card point count of only 9. But the Queen of Hearts assumes a somewhat greater value and we would regard the hand as somewhat better than 9 points in strength. It therefore becomes slightly too big for 1 No Trump.

2. A temporizing bid of 2 Clubs is in order. This hand is not quite strong enough for a 2 No Trump response, inasmuch as it has but 11 points in high cards, two short of the required number. However, you should arrange to make two bids with it; so a temporizing call is suggested. If partner repeats 2 Hearts, you then try 2 No Trump, which will designate a balanced hand containing 11 or 12 points.

3. **3 No Trump.** The exact size (16) and shape.

4. **2 No Trump.** You have 8 points in high cards.

5. **Pass.** In this balanced hand, containing but 4 points, there is no point in taking any action.

6. **3 Spades.** This hand has a high card equivalent of a raise to 3 No Trump (10 points); but since it is unbalanced, and may play better in Spades, the jump shift is suggested.

7. **3 Hearts.** Although this hand has no high card strength, it will surely play better in Hearts; and with a six card major we would insist upon playing it in that suit.

8. **3 Clubs.** To be followed by 6 No Trump, when partner bids 3 No Trump. This hand contains 14 points, so that the partnership is assured a minimum of 36 points. How-

ever, there may be a grand slam if partner has a maximum 2 No Trump opening. Remember, a response of 3 in a suit, followed by 6 No Trump, denotes a stronger hand than a direct leap to 6 No Trump.

9. 7 No Trump. You have 15 points in high cards, and even if partner has a minimum of 22, you will have 37. You are assured, therefore, that the opponents cannot have an Ace, and with a good five card suit, you should try for the big bonus.

QUIZ No. 5

1. 2 No Trump. Your hand has a high card count of 19, which demands a jump rebid, and all suits are accounted for.

2. 3 No Trump. This hand has a high card count of 21 points, without even considering the promoted value of the Jack of Spades. A jump to 3 No Trump is therefore indicated, describing a slightly stronger hand than the one on which opener makes a jump rebid of 2 No Trump, as in the previous example.

3. 1 No Trump. This hand contains only 15 points, and is, therefore, in the zone of minimum rebids.

4. Pass. This is a balanced hand of the No Trump family, and a five card suit should not be rebid in this situation. There is no hope for game as long as you own but 14 points and partner's maximum is 9; so it is not possible to approach the required 26 points.

5. 3 No Trump. With this evenly balanced hand, a rebid of the five card suit is not recommended. Such action might induce partner to try for the ten trick game. Holding only 12 points in high cards it is preferable to try for the nine trick game.

6. 2 Hearts. With this unbalanced hand, you should be able to play better at a suit. Game at No Trump is hopeless. Your hand for that purpose has a valuation of 15 points; but, when valued for suit play, it is worth 17 points. So, while there is no game in Spades or No Trump, there could conceivably be game at Hearts. Certainly Hearts may provide a safer part score contract.

7. 2 Hearts. In support of Hearts your hand is worth 15 points, 13 in high cards and 1 for each of the doubletons. A single raise is therefore clearly indicated.

8. 3 Hearts. In support of Hearts your hand is worth 19 points, 17 in high cards and 1 for each of the doubletons. When opener's hand is worth 19 points, he must make a jump rebid.

9. 3 Spades. You should make one try towards game. It is true that partner has announced a mediocre hand ranging somewhere between 6 and 10 points. If his hand has the value of 9 points, you should have a reasonable play for game. Your hand had an original valuation of 14 points, but when Spades were supported you must revalue the fifth and sixth trumps, adding 1 point for the fifth, and 2 points for the sixth. This gives your hand an adjusted value, after the raise, of 17 points. To put it in another way, your hand has somewhat over six probable winners. If partner can produce four, which normally takes about 9 or 10 points, you will have the ten required for game.

QUIZ No. 6

1. 3 No Trump. You have 13 points, and partner presumably has 13, so that the necessary 26 are in sight.

2. 1 Spade. It is true you have only 7 points in high cards, but the bid of 1 Spade should not be looked upon as another forward bid, since the contract is not being increased. You could hardly leave your partner in 1 Heart, nor return to 2 Clubs. Your alternate bid would be 1 No Trump, also an acceptable answer.

3. 3 Clubs. You are on the verge of a game and should try to determine whether 3 No Trump is available. Your hand has a value of 11 points, and partner's at least 14, so that you have a minimum of 25 points in the partnership assets.

4. Pass. You have a minimum 1 No Trump, of 16 points. Partner knows you have 16. It would, therefore, be highly improper for you to bid again. Partner's bid denotes a distributional holding with less than 10 points in high cards.

5. 3 Spades. Your hand has a value of only 12 points in support of Spades. This is normally 1 point short of the requirements for a jump raise; but, inasmuch as you have previously passed, you may take the liberty of jumping with a point less since partner need not go on if he does not choose to.

6. 1 Spade. This hand has a valuation of 9 points. It is not, therefore, strong enough to justify a redouble; nor would it be good strategy to pass and await developments, for the bidding might get too high the next time you had a chance to bid. At that time it might not be safe to show

your Spades. Remember, a bid over a double does not show weakness. It is a normal bid which merely denies the strength for a redouble.

7. 4 No Trump (Blackwood). Partner's response marks him with at least a six card suit headed by the Queen. The only question now is as to Aces. If partner has two of them you may calmly bid a grand slam. If he has one, you must be satisfied with a small slam. This is the easiest way to find out. The 4 No Trump bid in this sequence is an obvious Blackwood call.

8. 4 Hearts. This is an Ace showing bid, inasmuch as Spades are the agreed trump. If partner has the King of Hearts he should indicate it by a bid of 5 Hearts, in which case you may contract for slam.

9. 3 Diamonds. Your hand has a high card value of more than 11 points, for the Queen of Hearts is actually worth more than the 2 points assigned to it by the table. Since partner has shown distinctly more than an opening bid (16 points), it is quite plain that your side has the necessary 26 points for game; but while game in a minor suit might not be attainable, game in No Trump ought to be made if partner has Spades stopped. The correct call, therefore, is 3 Diamonds. If partner returns to 4 Clubs you may then decide to play for a minor suit game if you choose.

QUIZ No. 7

1. 6 Spades. Your hand had an original valuation of 20
   points, 19 in high cards and 1 for the doubleton. When
   the trump suit is supported, you must revalue your hand
   by adding another point for the fifth trump. That brings
   it up to 21. Partner has promised 13. The combined total
   is, therefore, at least 34. Partner's actual holding was:
   ♠ Q J x x x   ♡ A Q x   ◇ A J x   ♣ x x

2. 2 No Trump. You have a high card point count of 9, and
   the fact that you have no Spade stopper should not deter
   you from making your natural raise.

3. 2 No Trump. Your hand is worth 15 points in high cards,
   and partner's is worth at least 10 for the free bid of 1 No
   Trump. You should raise to 2, and if he has 11 or 12, he
   should go on.

4. 2 Spades. This hand has an actual value of only 9 points,
   10 in high cards, less a deduction of 1 for the 4-3-3-3
   distribution.

5. 2 Spades. This hand has a real value of only 9 points,
   7 in high cards, and 3 for the singleton Heart; but a deduction of a point must be made because you have only
   three trumps.

6. 3 Hearts. This hand is worth 14 points, 13 in high cards,
   and one for the doubleton Club.

7. Pass. Your hand is a minimum, having the valuation of
   13 points, 12 in high cards and 1 for the doubleton Diamond. Partner may not be relied upon for 13 points for
   if he had that many he would contract for game himself.
   Partner, therefore, has either 11 or 12.

8. 3 Hearts. This is preferable to rebidding Spades which would be improper strategy. Your hand has a valuation of 16 points in support of Hearts, and a raise is therefore mandatory. A rebid of 2 Spades would be a denial of such strength. While it is tempting to bid 4 Hearts, remember opener should not make a jump rebid with only 16 points.

9. Redouble. Despite the fact that you have no support for Hearts, the 12 points in high cards justifies such action. The opponents are in trouble; and if partner passes the next call around to you, you will be in position to double them.

QUIZ No. 8

1. 1 No Trump. This hand has a high card count of 18,
    with balanced distribution, and a 1 No Trump bid is
    much preferable to a call of 1 Diamond. There is a dis-
    tinct advantage to being declarer on this hand for the
    opening lead in all suits will likely be to your advantage.
    If you open with 1 Diamond, you will have a very dif-
    ficult rebid if partner should respond with 1 Spade, for
    the hand will be slightly.short of a 2 No Trump rebid
    and much too good for a discouraging rebid of Diamonds.

2. 2 Spades. This hand has a high card count (8 points) for
    a raise to 2 No Trump. But this unbalanced hand may
    play better in a major suit, so that a 2 Spade bid is pre-
    ferred. If partner raises to 3, it is your intention to con-
    tract for game in Spades. If he rebids 2 No Trump, you
    may go on to 3. If he passes, it will mean that he has but
    16 points and that game will not be a bright prospect.

3. At this point you should make a bid that is forcing to
    game. Holding 21 points in high cards you would have
    rebid 3 No Trump if partner had responded with 1 Dia-
    mond; but such a call is not acceptable with an unpro-
    tected suit. A jump to game in Hearts would be irregular
    with only three trumps; so an artificial jump shift is rec-
    ommended—namely, 2 Spades. This jump in a new suit is
    forcing to game, and your next move will depend on part-
    ner's rebid.

4. A jump in Clubs is indicated since partner has shown a
    holding of six Clubs and five Spades. On the basis of
    values you have sufficient to contract for 6 Clubs, but
    there is a slight danger of duplication. Partner might
    be void in Diamonds, and hold two losing Hearts, which

would be the case if he held six good Clubs, five solid Spades and the King and one Diamond. The recommended bid is, therefore, 5 Clubs; and if partner controls the Heart suit he will be in a position to contract for slam.

5. The proper procedure is a forcing pass. Your opening 2 Spade bid committed your partnership to game; and a pass by you at this point is just as forcing as a bid. It must be recollected that partner denied any high card strength, and you have a slightly shaded 2 bid. The advantage of the pass is that partner may have considerable values in Clubs and be in a position to punish East's overcall severely. If he is unable to double the 3 Club bid he is obliged to proceed and you will then contract for game. Furthermore, he may have a mild Club stopper and be in a position to bid 3 No Trump, which might be the only makable game.

6. Pass. You have a high card count of 7, which means a very mediocre holding. Had the fourth hand passed, you would have kept the bidding open; but in this sequence there is no advantage in acting. You should make it easy for the opponents to bid, for anything they bid will be to your taste. We do not sympathize with the panicky feeling that induces a rescue in this situation. If you pass, the opponents will almost invariably take this right off your hands.

7. Pass. There is no possible chance for game. You have only 13 points in high cards, and partner cannot possibly have that much else he would have jumped in No Trump on the second round. No thought should be given to rebidding Clubs. Since all suits are accounted for, the best place to play this indifferent hand is at 1 No Trump.

8. Pass. An overcall of 2 Clubs would not be safe. This hand
    could easily produce only four tricks in the play, and you
    are contracting for eight. The risk is unjustified, particu-
    larly with a passing partner, and game quite out of the
    question. You could easily lose more than two trump
    tricks.

9. 2 No Trump. While it is true that this hand has the value
    of 10 points in support of Spades, and will be very
    helpful to partner, the technical response of 2 No Trump
    must be made on any hand that does not contain a de-
    fensive (quick) trick. On the next round you should
    jump in Spades to indicate that while you lack the honor
    strength, you have great distributional support.

A SUMMARY OF THE GOREN POINT COUNT METHOD OF CONTRACT BIDDING

THE POINT COUNT TABLE

ACE = 4 POINTS

KING = 3 POINTS

QUEEN = 2 POINTS

JACK = 1 POINT

26 points will normally produce game. (For a minor suit game 29 points will be required.)

33 points will normally produce a small slam.

37 points will normally produce a grand slam.

Opening Bids of One in a Suit

In opening bids of 1 in a suit the value of a hand is determined by computing the high cards held and adding:

3 points for a void

2 points for each singleton

1 point for each doubleton

12 point hands may be opened if there is a *good rebid* and they contain two quick tricks.

13 point hands are optional openings. Bid them if convenient.

14 point hands *must* be opened.

A third hand opening may be made with 11 points, or even a little less, if a fairly good suit is held.

A fourth hand opening should be made on 13 points, even though no good rebid is available.

An Opening Demand Bid of Two in a Suit Requires:

> A good five card suit with a minimum of 25 points
> A good six card suit with a minimum of 23 points
> A good seven card suit with a minimum of 21 points

Do not make an opening pre-emptive bid on any hand containing as many as 11 points (exclusive of distribution).

Opening No Trump Bids Count High Card Values Only. No Points Are Given for Distribution.

> Opening 1 No Trump—16 to 18 points
> Opening 2 No Trump—22 to 24 points
> Opening 3 No Trump—25 to 27 points

Responses to Opening 1 No Trump Bids:

Raise to 2 No Trump with 8 or 9 points (or 7 points with a five card suit)

Raise to 3 No Trump with 10 to 14 points

Raise to 4 No Trump with 15 or 16 points

Raise to 6 No Trump with 17 or 18 points

Bid 3 of a suit, then 6 No Trump with 19 or 20 points

Raise to 7 No Trump with 21 points

A response of 2 Clubs or 2 Diamonds shows less than 7 points

A response of 2 Hearts or 2 Spades may contain as many as 8 or 9 points, but shows a five card suit and an unbalanced hand

A response of 4 Spades or 4 Hearts shows a long suit (six or seven cards) with less than 10 points in high cards

A response of 3 in any suit shows a hand with 10 or more points and a good suit

Responses to 2 No Trump Bids:

Raise to 3 No Trump with 4 to 8 points

Raise to 4 No Trump with 9 points

Bid 3 of a suit and then 4 No Trump with 10 points

Raise to 6 No Trump with 11 or 12 points

Bid 3 of a suit, then 6 No Trump, with 13 or 14 points

Raise to 7 No Trump with 15 points

With a five card major suit headed by an honor, and 4 points, bid that suit at the level of 3

Show any six card major suit

Don't bother to show minor suits unless you contemplate a slam

Responses to 3 No Trump Bids:

Raise to 4 No Trump with 7 points

Raise to 6 No Trump with 8 or 9 points

Bid 4 Diamonds, then 6 No Trump with 10 or 11 points

Raise to 7 No Trump with 12 points

Show any five card suit if the hand contains 5 points in high cards

In Making Suit Responses Add the Distributional Points to High Card Values. Table of Valuation for Dummy Hand in Raising Partner's Suit Bid:

(A) Count high cards at face value

(B) Promote honors in partner's suit

(C) Add 1 point for each doubleton
        3 points for each singleton
        5 points for a void

(D) Deduct 1 point if your hand contains only three trumps
        1 point if your hand is distributed 4-3-3-3

Respond 1 No Trumps with 6 to 9 points

Respond 2 No Trump with 13 to 15 points

Respond 3 No Trump with 16 to 18 points

Raise partner's suit bid to 2 with 6 to 10 points

Raise partner's suit bid to 3 with 13 to 16 points

Make a jump shift with 19 points

Show a new suit at 1 level with 6 points

Show a new suit at 2 level with 10 points

With hands counting 11 or 12 points find two bids without forcing partner to game.

The Take-Out Double

A take-out double should be based on a hand of the same strength as an opening bid, that is, 13 points for a double of a suit bid.

An immediate double of 1 No Trump therefore should be based on 16 points.

When partner responds in a suit for which you have good support, revalue your hand as dummy.

As responder to a take-out double: if you have 6 points you have a fair hand, 9 points a good hand, and 11 points a probable game.

As partner of the opening bidder, after a take-out double, pass with a poor hand, redouble with a good hand, and bid immediately with a moderate hand.